SUBSTANCE USE, MISUSE AND RELAPSE IN THE ADDICTIONS TREATMENT WORKFORCE

ISSUES AND SOLUTIONS

SUBSTANCE ABUSE ASSESSMENT, INTERVENTIONS AND TREATMENT

Additional books in this series can be found on Nova's website under the Series tab.

Additional E-books in this series can be found on Nova's website under the E-book tab.

SUBSTANCE ABUSE ASSESSMENT, INTERVENTIONS AND TREATMENT

SUBSTANCE USE, MISUSE AND RELAPSE IN THE ADDICTIONS TREATMENT WORKFORCE

ISSUES AND SOLUTIONS

JONAS EISENSTADT
EDITOR

nova
publishers
New York

Library of Congress Cataloging-in-Publication Data

ISBN: 978-1-62808-646-1

Published by Nova Science Publishers, Inc. † New York

CONTENTS

PREFACE

Like all professions, the addictions treatment field is faced with the challenges of employee substance use and abuse and their impact on retention of quality staff. Because the addictions field employs a disproportionate number of individuals – by recent estimates close to half of the treatment workforce – in recovery, the field faces particular retention challenges. This book provides meaningful and practical guidance to the problem of substance misuse among addictions professionals. The treatment field presents a professional environment where triggers for relapse are present. The ability to support employees through prevention and intervention and with access to treatment and recovery support services is critical to retaining a workforce that can bring richness and personal experience to the workplace, while maintaining its dedication to providing quality services to its clients.

Chapter 1 – Report of the Substance Abuse and Mental Health Services Administration's Center for Substance Abuse Treatment, under the Partners for Recovery Initiative, on Supporting Our Greatest Resource: Addressing Substance Use, Misuse and Relapse in the Addiction Treatment Workforce.

Chapter 2 – Report of the Central East Addiction Technology Transfer Center, on Self Care: A Guide for Addiction Professionals dated October 2011.

In: Substance Use, Misuse and Relapse ...   ISBN: 978-1-62808-646-1
Editor: Jonas Eisenstadt   © 2013 Nova Science Publishers, Inc.

Chapter 1

SUPPORTING OUR GREATEST RESOURCE: ADDRESSING SUBSTANCE USE, MISUSE AND RELAPSE IN THE ADDICTION TREATMENT WORKFORCE[*]

Eve Weinberg and Tim Whitney

I. INTRODUCTION

Like all professions, the addictions treatment field is faced with the challenges of employee substance use and abuse and their impact on retention of quality staff. Because the addictions field employees a disproportionate number of individuals – by recent estimates close to half of the treatment workforce – in recovery, the field faces particular retention challenges. This toolkit provides meaningful and practical guidance to the problem of substance misuse among addictions professionals. The treatment field presents a professional environment where triggers for relapse are present. The ability to support employees through prevention and intervention and with access to treatment and recovery support services is critical to retaining a workforce that can bring richness and personal experience to the workplace, while maintaining its dedication to providing quality services to its clients.

---

[*] This is an edited, reformatted and augmented version of the Substance Abuse and Mental Health Services Administration's Center for Substance Abuse Treatment, under the Partners for Recovery Initiative, dated ___ .

This toolkit is designed for provider organizations in the addictions field, their executives, managers and human resources staff. It includes practical resources and information to guide and assist providers as they face workforce issues associated with substance use, misuse and recovery among employees. More broadly, it will assist employers in creating a work environment that supports the needs of employees, engages and retains employees in the addictions field, and in the case of use, misuse and relapse, intervenes in a way that is effective while being legally and corporately responsible.

Background

Substance misuse – the misuse of legal (including alcohol and prescriptions medication) and illegal drugs – is a problem for all industries. The addictions treatment and recovery field is not immune. In fact, given the over- representation of people in recovery in the treatment workforce and the potential for relapse among recovering individuals it can be assumed that the addictions treatment field may experience more problems related to substance misuse than other fields. And generally speaking, a stressed and overworked workforce is always at risk for a variety of problems, including substance use or misuse. Corporate symptoms of these issues may include high turnover and low retention rates, which in turn result in higher training costs and greater human resources expenses associated with recruiting and record-keeping. Most importantly, the inability to retain staff severely hampers an agency's ability to consistently deliver high-caliber treatment and recovery services.

In 2007, the Substance Abuse and Mental Health Services Administration, Center for Substance Abuse Treatment (SAMHSA/CSAT) released a report titled *Strengthening Professional Identity: Challenges of the Addictions Treatment Workforce*. This report noted that "Clinicians face the reality of relapse every day in managing patients/clients, but many treatment agencies are not well prepared to address relapse within their own staff." The report also observed that "many organizations lack policies and resources that assist supervisors in taking appropriate action when impairment is detected." The report recommended developing strategies and policies related to substance use, misuse, relapse and wellness for the addictions field

Certainly, employee wellness and retention are not the only issues facing the treatment workforce. Other issues, such as recruitment, pay scales, benefits and professionalism, also play a role, but they are beyond the purview of this document. The tools presented here focus on the challenges facing workers in the addictions field that underlie the retention crisis. Members of the workforce who are in recovery have a wealth of experience that makes them effective clinicians. At the same time, however, they often face situations that place them at high risk for use, misuse and relapse. To combat these underlying issues and improve retention, agencies in the field need effective wellness policies and practices that address the unique challenges these employees face.

Recovery and Retention in the Workplace

It has often been stated that when talking about retention problems in the addictions workforce, the "elephant in the room" is the fact that a large percentage of the workforce is in recovery and therefore vulnerable to relapse. An environmental scan conducted by SAMSHA and Abt Associates in 2003 estimated that almost 50% of the workforce in private treatment was in recovery. The nature of addiction as a chronic disease in which relapse is common requires first and foremost that any wellness program for the field effectively addresses relapse, intervention and prevention.

Many people in the addictions treatment workforce, both those in recovery and those not in recovery, face challenges that compromise their ability to maintain employment and provide quality services. It is counterproductive to believe that staff can "leave their issues at the door" when they arrive at work in the morning. The reality is that these issues follow staff into the workplace and affect service quality as well as employee retention.

All staff can benefit from addictions prevention and wellness programs. Prevention and intervention are important components of workforce retention efforts.

Opportunities for the Field

The addictions treatment field has many innate features that make it uniquely able to incorporate effective prevention and intervention technologies into workplace policies and practices. These features include corporate missions related to recovery from addictive diseases; strong corporate cultures that forbid the use of substances; strong codes of ethics regarding the use and abuse of substances; and awareness of treatment, prevention and recovery support resources in the field and community.

Perhaps the field's greatest strength in dealing with employee addiction is the natural expertise of staff and management in recognizing and responding to substance use. While it is true that not everyone who works at a treatment agency is a trained clinician, every agency certainly possesses the core skills needed to address use, misuse and relapse.

Managers in the addictions treatment and recovery field walk a fine line when it comes to dealing with staff who may be experiencing problems related to substance misuse. They know how to use their skills to manage and supervise staff, but common wisdom says that managers should not take on the role of clinician and should not diagnose or treat their own staff. They can, however, carefully observe workplace behaviors and use their observational skills to note potential problems before they become more severe. They also can use their subject matter expertise and their knowledge of the community to design and implement appropriate, responsive and responsible strategies to address use and misuse among employees. Some of the clinical skills that can be applied in a managerial and supervisory context and that serve as the foundation for many of the tools and resources presented here include:

- Observing Staff
- Providing Feedback
- Adapting Appropriate Confrontation
- Increasing Motivation to Change
- Making Referrals to Services
- Establishing Behavioral Contracting
- Requiring Accountability
- Measuring Progress

Currently, the field is not adequately using these capabilities to prevent staff relapse or misuse or to intervene effectively when these issues arise. There are many reasons for this, not the least of which is concern that confronting the problem will violate various employment laws. Treatment providers may be inclined to immediately terminate staff members who relapse or show early signs of potential relapse. Although this approach is entirely logical and reasonable from a corporate risk-management perspective, it exacerbates retention problems. Immediate termination often means loss of staff members who, with help and appropriate support, could continue to contribute to their employer and the field. Additionally, this approach runs counter to what is known about addiction and recovery – that addiction is a chronic disease and recovery is a lifelong process to be managed.

How can treatment centers create workplace policies that protect themselves and their clients while simultaneously supporting staff who may be experiencing difficulties? In other words, how do centers responsibly and ethically align corporate and clinical values? By combining best practices in human resources, addictions clinical practice, and management policies and practices, corporate and clinical values can be aligned and turnover reduced, high performers retained and staff performance improved. This toolkit aims to provide practical tools – workplace policies, procedures, practices and tips for supervisors – that allow the addictions treatment and recovery field to legally, ethically and effectively help prevent substance misuse among its workers and to intervene appropriately when it occurs. The overall goal of the toolkit is to allow agencies to support wellness among their employees, increase retention of their valued workers and ultimately provide a consistently high caliber of services to their clients.

While many of the arguments for development of retention-oriented practices in the addictions field are presented here in an ethical and/or philosophical context, the fiscal context also deserves mention. Conservative estimates of the cost of employee turnover are 25% to 30% of an employee's salary – a cost that the historically under-funded addictions treatment field can ill-afford to assume. Simply stated, there is a financial benefit to retaining quality staff. This benefit is realized in reduced training and administrative costs for new employees and in greater efficiencies in service delivery.

Ethical Considerations

As companies, providers must learn to balance the realities of the issues staff face with corporate risk-management responsibilities. Ethically, the field cannot create policies that allow or encourage managers to become therapists or counselors for their staff. Ethical boundaries must be clearly delineated and maintained between supervisors and managers and their employees. At the same time, staff members who should not be providing services must be restricted from providing care. There may be circumstances in which an employee is removed from face-to-face interaction with clients and in which termination is the most appropriate course of action. Good policies and practices concerning these issues can teach managers how to appropriately identify potential staff problems early on and can give them the resources they need to effectively deal with problems before they threaten an employee's job or the quality of client service.

Introduction to the Toolkit

The effort that resulted in this toolkit is but part of a growing national awareness of and attention to the seriousness of employee substance misuse. In particular, the Addiction Technology Transfer Centers (ATTCs) have enhanced the field's overall understanding of use, misuse and wellness among the workforce, including implications and opportunities for solutions. In 2007, the Central East ATTC published *Self Care: A Guide for Addiction Professionals*, which laid out guidelines for employers and employees to promote overall wellness. Also in 2007, the Southeast ATTC published symposium proceedings titled *Alcohol and Other Drug Problems Among Addiction Professionals*. This report highlighted 12 elements – including collecting needs assessment data, establishing Employee Assistance Program (EAP) standards, providing training, and establishing policies and practices – as critical to holistically and successfully addressing the problem. The tools presented here follow in the footsteps of and are guided by these efforts. The toolkit includes policies, tools and resources for use by agency clinical supervisors and managers, executive directors, residents, boards of directors and human resources professionals.

Process

The toolkit reflects the contributions of a Steering Committee composed of leaders and experts in the addictions field. These individuals represent a wide range of perspectives and areas of experience, including provider agencies, State administration, association-level leadership, insurance and medicine. What they all share is the desire to maintain a quality workforce delivering quality services in light of the serious challenges facing the addictions treatment field.

The Steering Committee in framing the purpose of the toolkit identified three paradoxes that must be addressed related to wellness and the retention of employees in use, misuse and relapse situations. The paradoxes are:

Paradox 1: Clinical Values vs. Corporate Values. How providers approach use and misuse among employees does not always mirror how providers approach use and misuse among clients. This discrepancy reveals a contradiction between corporate values and clinical practices. Providers premise client services on a belief in personal recovery and an understanding of the complex lifelong nature of recovery and the potential for relapse. Providers know how to effectively intervene with clients, applying the latest science, evidence-based practices and other new learning from the field. That same philosophy, however, is not carried over to staff. In use, misuse or relapse situations, staff members may be disciplined or even terminated without any effort to engage them in intervention, treatment or recovery support. Providers should be given the tools needed to apply their knowledge to create and foster a work environment where individuals feel comfortable stating there is a problem, where intervention can happen and where support systems can be accessed.

Paradox 2: Richness of Service Delivery vs. Employee Vulnerability. Many people enter the treatment field as a result of personal experiences with recovery, either their own or someone else's. While these experiences encourage them to help others in similar circumstances and bring depth and richness to service delivery, they also result in a staff that is disproportionately more vulnerable to the daily realities of working with addicted populations. Employers are challenged to balance the value of personal experience in service delivery with stressors that promote relapse. For example, a counselor in recovery who has served time for drug-related crimes could be an invaluable asset to a post-release group-treatment process, but exposing that counselor to the emotions, attitudes and circumstances of that time in his life could serve as a trigger for relapse. Agencies need the tools and resources to encourage participation of employees with personal recovery experiences while minimizing the risk of their exposure to stressors that may promote use, misuse or relapse.

Paradox 3: Clinical Skills vs. Management Skills. Lack of appropriate managerial training, support, and policies and procedures contributes to providers' overall inability to align clinical and corporate values. Managers may have excellent skills but inadequate knowledge, tools and practice on how to use those skills in context. As a result, they may fear making a human resources "mistake," which leads to an employee complaint or lawsuit. This fear is encouraged by human resources professionals and employment law attorneys who counsel managers to avoid any conversations regarding the roots of performance problems and focus solely on workplace performance issues. Fear also may lead to immediate referrals to outside services such as EAPs without any internal discussions about how to properly support the employee. Managers need tools and training to provide them with legal, ethical and effective ways to talk to and intervene with staff – regarding the root causes of performance problems without breaching legal or ethical boundaries.

The Steering Committee identified the following priorities and supporting activities to provide guidance regarding products that should be included in the toolkit:

Priority 1: Creating a healthy work culture to support employee wellness and retention.

- Employers should create a corporate culture that acknowledges the reality of employee use and misuse of alcohol and drugs and be prepared to address those challenges. At the highest levels – executive staff, boards of advisors and directors – each employer must articulate a vision for support that will permeate all corporate policies and practices.
- Employers should integrate support, prevention and early intervention models into management strategies. These models will encourage, offer and/or link to opportunities for peer support, general recovery support and wellness activities for employees both in recovery and not in recovery.

Priority 2: Creating processes for addressing use and misuse to facilitate recovery and wellness among employees.

- Employers should develop policies for dealing with employee use, misuse, relapse and reintegration situations, including personnel and management tools such as scripts and guidelines. Good policies and practices can teach managers to identify potential staff problems early on and give them the resources they need to effectively deal with problems before they threaten an employee's job or quality services to clients.

Misconduct vs. Gross Misconduct

This toolkit provides resources to *appropriately intervene* with staff members who struggle with substance misuse and recovery. The primary responsibility of the field is the safety and health of clients. As a result, the definition of "appropriate intervention" must be viewed through the lens of impact on client service. Therefore, in determining employee interventions it is important to distinguish between "misconduct" vs. "gross misconduct."

When an addictions professional misuses substances (whether he or she is in recovery or not), job performance is generally compromised. Often, before the misuse or relapse escalates, there are workplace performance problems that might indicate relapse or misuse has occurred. (Many of these performance problems are outlined in the section below, "Behavioral Red Flags: Appropriate Supervision Intervention Points.")

There is no single accepted definition of either misconduct or gross misconduct. Generally speaking, misconduct is action, inaction or behavior that is a violation of work rules and grounds for intervention discipline and potentially discharge. Gross misconduct is generally behavior that is more serious than misconduct and constitutes grounds for immediate dismissal without prior warning or discipline. Precise definitions can vary between workplaces. For example, gross misconduct has been defined as conduct that gives rise to a clear and present danger to health and safety and as behavior that is disruptive to operations and hostile and intimidating to other employees.

Sometimes substance misuse leads to gross misconduct. Gross misconduct should not be tolerated, regardless of the underlying cause. Staff members who engage in gross misconduct should face disciplinary action up to and including immediate termination. Misconduct, on the other hand, is behavior that should be addressed and modified but does not necessarily rise to the level of termination. In the case of misconduct, managerial responses can include both behavioral intervention and disciplinary action. For example, a staff member could receive a written warning (disciplinary action) and also be referred to the EAP (intervention). There may also be instances of repeated misconduct wherein, while no single incident rises to the level of gross misconduct, the pattern of behavior suggests disciplinary action up to and including termination.

The table that follows provides examples of misconduct versus gross misconduct. This list is not meant to be exhaustive but merely illustrative of some common workplace issues.

Misconduct	Gross Misconduct
Taking a client to her son's basketball game	Engaging in a sexual relationship with a client
Letting certification lapse, but informing the agency	Knowingly misrepresenting one's credentials
Drinking alcohol at a professional conference	Using drugs or alcohol with a client
Being charged with a DUI on a Saturday night and reporting it to a supervisor on Monday morning	Driving clients to appointments while under the influence of drugs or alcohol
Failing to turn in a report to the court on time	Lying in reports to the court about a client's drug-free status
Yelling at a client in a group session	Threatening a client with unsuccessful termination if she refuses to engage in a sexual relationship with the counselor
Failing to document services that were provided	Falsifying documentation to reflect client services that were not rendered
Missing a routine client meeting	Failing to answer the phone calls of a client in crisis

Substance Misuse Does not Discriminate Based on Job Title

This toolkit lays out various prevention, intervention and reintegration strategies that can be used in the addictions workplace. Because the majority of employees in the field are clinical staff, the majority of the toolkit is written as though the employee with the substance misuse issue provides direct clinical services. The employee doing the intervening is described as a supervisor. It is important to note, however, that substance misuse can and does occur at all levels of the organization and thus that intervention must be provided at all levels as well.

Additionally, quality intervention is never a one-person job. When substance misuse occurs in the workforce, it is vitally important that agency executives, decision- makers, risk managers, human resources staff and legal counsel provide consultation, supervision and guidance as their roles, responsibilities and expertise dictate.

II. GENERAL GUIDELINE

Please Note: The resources, tools and other information presented in this toolkit are offered as guidance for treatment provider agencies use.

They are designed to be as universally applicable as possible. While every attempt has been made to ensure they meet legal requirements, they should not be substituted for independent legal counsel. Additional local, State and Federal laws may apply.

Workplace Policies: A Framework for Understanding the Role of Tools, Policies and Procedures

Resources, policies and procedures in this toolkit include components of one or more of the following concepts:

- **Prevention:** How can employers help prevent relapse or substance misuse in a vulnerable workforce?
- **Intervention:** How can employers effectively intervene when relapse or misuse occurs?
- **Re-entry:** How can employers' help those who have relapsed or who have had misuse interfere with their work re-enter the workplace after an appropriate intervention?

These three concepts represent the scope of action that an agency can take to support its employees. Some policies may include elements of all three concepts; some may include elements of only one. All three concepts must be brought to bear in developing a holistic set of policies focused on employee wellness and retention. The philosophies underlying each of these concepts are discussed in more detail below.

It must be noted here that the agency's goal is always optimum service delivery to *clients* through a quality and stable workforce.

Prevention: A Lesson from Universal Precautions
In the context of this toolkit, prevention is viewed very broadly as minimizing the circumstances under which an employee may use or misuse substances. Resources and policies within the prevention category are intended to apply to *all* staff. Critical legal and ethical questions arise when prevention efforts are targeted to specific staff in recovery. The concept of universal precautions is illustrative in this regard. As a paramedic assumes *by default*

that every patient has a potentially communicable disease, prevention policies that aim to reduce substance misuse in the workplace also should assume *by default* that the whole staff may, at some point, be at risk for substance misuse that might affect performance or job retention. Thus, prevention-related policies should be aimed at the whole workforce, regardless of recovery status.

Intervention: Opening the Door

Once an employee has shown symptoms of relapse or misuse, supervisors and managers should intervene appropriately with workplace policies and tools designed to support the intervention. Policies should clearly state that the agency will endeavor to provide reasonable support to staff members who experience substance misuse problems and who self-report such issues, *as long as the impairment has not led to serious issues of misconduct.*

A formal policy that encourages employees to self-report relapse or misuse issues to their supervisor is fundamental to the ability to intervene quickly and effectively. Employees are more likely to self-report problems if they feel they will be supported and if they feel that not reporting and continuing to use might lead to more serious consequences. Examples of supportive intervention policies include:

- Policies that allow employees to take a leave of absence during which they seek treatment or other appropriate services
- Job security policies that allow a job to be held for a period of time for employees who go to treatment
- Health insurance policies that include good substance abuse benefits
- Disability insurance (or other benefits) that allows some salary replacement while an employee is out on approved leave
- A strong and visible EAP

Re-Entry and Reintegration: Encouraging and Promoting Retention

Where appropriate, intervention strategies should be designed with a return to full job responsibilities as the ultimate goal. The tools, policies and resources in this toolkit are separate from general intervention strategies, although in most cases, they will be applied in concert. In many ways, a return-to-work plan resembles a recovery plan, with defined activities, standards, goals, guidelines, benchmarks, rewards and sanctions to manage the process.

Corporate Commitment to Employee Wellness

Establishing a corporate culture that supports employee wellness and retention begins at the top level of an organization with the leadership and board of directors, particularly in a workplace with a unique vulnerability to substance use and misuse. Organizational policies and actions should convey that the agency takes employee substance use and misuse very seriously but operates on the belief that recovery is a reality that should be available not only to clients but to staff as well.

Below are three documents organizations can use to establish employee wellness as a priority. The first document is a Corporate Commitment Policy that should be incorporated into the employee policy manual and presented in new-staff training. The second document is a Board Resolution that raises the substance use and misuse issue to the highest level of organization management and becomes a permanent part of the agency's leadership record. The third document is a series of talking points that agency leaders can use when communicating with partners and contractors, such as accountants, management entities, attorneys and other service providers. This document asserts the organization's belief in the importance of employee wellness.

These documents contain overlapping concepts and language, including:

- Prioritization of and fidelity to quality client services
- Acknowledgement of the unique vulnerabilities of the addictions workforce
- Assertion of the importance of facilitating access to care for employees, while not jeopardizing client services
- A clear presentation of the options available to employees regarding treatment and other support

---

SAMPLE CORPORATE COMMITMENT POLICY

Company XYZ is an addictions treatment agency. Our corporate mission is to help our clients suffering from addictive disease learn to manage their disease and maintain recovery. Our primary responsibility is to that mission. At all times, our paramount concern is the safety and well-being of the clients who have entrusted us to help guide them in their recovery process.

From time to time, our employees also may face problems related to substance use and misuse. As outlined in our Drug Testing, Professional Conduct and, when applicable, Drug-Free Workplace policies, employees may not work at Company XYZ while they are misusing substances. Impaired employees put themselves, our clients, other employees, and the reputation and mission of our organization at risk.

Our fundamental belief in the power of recovery and individual behavior change dictates that we establish workplace policies and practices that help prevent substance misuse among our employees; intervene appropriately when misuse occurs; and, when possible and appropriate. help staff members who have experienced misuse problems successfully return to work.

We encourage employees who experience substance misuse problems to seek appropriate help quickly. To assist them, we have instituted workplace policies and practices that align our corporate values with our clinical mission. They include:

- Health insurance that covers substance abuse and mental health services
- A strong EAP where employees can receive confidential services
- Disability insurance that provides some salary replacement for those who go to treatment
- Sick time policies that allow for time off to receive necessary services
- Leave polices that allow eligible employees to take time off from work to pursue treatment or other recovery support services
- Return-to-work policies to help employees return to their jobs when they are ready and that outline the conditions under which employees can return to work
- A list of peer assistance programs in our area

We strongly encourage employees who are experiencing substance misuse problems to talk to their supervisor, manager or human resources director. In cases where there is misuse but no serious misconduct or other performance problems that rise to the level of termination, it may be possible to arrange for a leave of absence and a tailored return-to-work plan appropriate for the circumstances.

SAMPLE BOARD RESOLUTION

We, the Directors of Company XYZ, hereby resolve the following:

- That the corporate mission of Company XYZ is to help our clients suffering from addictive disease learn to manage their disease and maintain recovery, and that our primary responsibility is to that mission, and;
- That because of the nature of our work, the pressures of the addictions treatment environment and the proportion of employees who may be in recovery, we also must encourage employees encountering problems related to substance use and misuse to seek assistance, and;
- That our fundamental belief in the power of recovery and individual behavior change dictates that we institute workplace policies and practices that help prevent substance misuse among our employees; intervene appropriately when misuse occurs; and, when possible and appropriate, help staff who have experienced misuse problems successfully return to work, and;
- That support for employee treatment and recovery will occur alongside disciplinary action resulting from any misconduct or inability to meet job responsibilities stemming from substance use and misuse, and;
- That even in cases where substance use, misuse and related conduct results in termination, we will encourage employees to seek treatment and refer them to the appropriate resources.

Red Flags That Staff May be Misusing Substances

Introduction

One of the key skills that can be brought to bear on the issue of use and misuse among staff is the observation of behaviors that may indicate use. This section provides examples of workplace behaviors that may suggest use by an employee and suggests responses or resources from the toolkit that may be applicable. In some cases, these behaviors, or a combination of them, may serve as probable cause for drug testing.

Unexplained Absenteeism

Employees who might be experiencing relapse or misuse problems will likely experience increased *unplanned* absences. Unplanned time off usually presents itself as sick time. The employee might call in sick more frequently or show a pattern of calling in sick to extend planned time off such as holidays or weekends. Other patterns of unexplained absenteeism that may indicate a problem include being absent the day after payday or coming in on payday for a check and then leaving.

SAMPLE TALKING POINTS FOR AGENCY LEADERSHIP

- Our corporate mission is to help our clients suffering from addictive disease learn to manage their disease and maintain recovery, and our primary responsibility is to that mission. At all times, the safety and well-being of our clients is our paramount concern.
- Because of the nature of our work, the pressures of the addictions treatment environment and the proportion of employees who may be in recovery, we also must recognize the unique vulnerabilities of our staff and encourage employees encountering problems related to their own substance use and misuse to seek assistance,
- Our fundamental belief in the power of recovery and individual behavior change dictates that we establish workplace policies and practices that help prevent substance misuse among our employees; intervene appropriately when misuse occurs; and when possible and appropriate, help staff who have experienced misuse problems successfully return to work.
- Employees may not work at our company while they are misusing substances. Impaired employees put themselves, our clients, other employees, and the reputation and mission of our organization at risk.
- To align our corporate values with our clinical mission, we have employed the following policies:
  - Health insurance that covers substance abuse and mental health services
  - A strong EAP where employees can receive confidential services

---

- Disability insurance that provides some salary replacement for those who go to treatment
- Sick time policies that allow for time off to receive necessary services
- Leave polices that allow eligible employees to take time off from work to pursue treatment or other recovery support services
- Return-to-work policies to help employees return to their jobs when they are ready and that outline the conditions under which employees can return to work
- A list of peer assistance programs in our area

The Response: A sick time policy that incorporates these considerations is included here in section in III. Organizational Policies.

Abuse of Work Hours

Employees experiencing substance use problems often have difficulties meeting scheduled responsibilities. These difficulties may manifest as tardiness, long lunches, and frequent breaks or unaccounted for time. The treatment environment also presents opportunities for extended time "in the field," such as site or home visits.

The Response: Supervisors should look for these behaviors and intervene quickly. When patterns of behavior emerge, the supervisor should point out to the employee that he or she has observed the employee's problem. The supervisor should point out that these behaviors decrease the employee's effectiveness and are not acceptable. Employees should be monitored and reminded about the EAP. The supervisor can state that sometimes issues in one's personal life can lead to absenteeism, tardiness and a general lack of accountability. An Hours of Work Policy that incorporates these considerations is included in this toolkit.

Finances

As substance issues get worse, financial problems often follow. Financial trouble may manifest itself when employees borrow money from co-workers, pad expense reports or ask for paychecks in advance. An increase in wage assignments and garnishments also may indicate that an employee is experiencing financial pressure.

The Response: Supervisors should be aware that these problems can indicate misuse or relapse. Employees who experience these problems should be advised to seek financial counseling, a service that many EAPs provide. Except for clear cases of expense report abuse, these issues are generally not covered by specific policies. As a result, supervisors must be particularly vigilant in observing and responding to them.

Productivity and Effectiveness

Substance use often results in a marked change in employee productivity. It is important to note that an unexpected *increase* in activity, such as reporting increased service hours, may be as indicative of a problem as a decrease in productivity. Substance abuse also is likely to interfere with effectiveness in the work setting. Supervisors should know that changes in productivity and effectiveness can signal substance misuse and should be aware of marked positive and negative changes in both areas.

The Response: Productivity and effectiveness are generally not covered by specific policies; therefore, management and clinical supervision are key to recognizing problems in these areas.

Quality Assurance

Quality assurance encompasses a wide range of activities, including actual service delivery, record keeping, and relationships with peers and others. Problems with service quality may manifest as client complaints, errors in record keeping or missing records, complaints from co-workers, and general behavior in the workplace.

The Response: Supervision is important, including announced and unannounced employee observation in the service delivery setting and regular file reviews. A quality assurance policy that incorporates these considerations is included as part of the toolkit.

Guidelines, Tips and Scripts for Clinical Supervision

The Importance of Quality Supervision

Frequent, focused and attentive clinical supervision is one of the keys to prevention of substance misuse, effective intervention and successful employee re-entry into the workforce.

This section includes some tips, scripts and talking points for supervisors to use when responding to actual or potential use or misuse among employees. What follows are guidelines and examples of true-life scenarios that demonstrate the role of the supervisor, the role of clinical supervision, some challenges and pitfalls associated with supervision, and suggestions for overcoming these obstacles. These guidelines should be applied as appropriate for the individual workplace. Supervisory relationships can be used appropriately when structure and policies exist to support intervention.

The Preventive Role: What Organizations Should Say to Staff about Use and Misuse

When training staff and in day-to-day managerial settings, it is important to adopt a preventive mindset that acknowledges that use and misuse are ever-present concerns and that the organization actively supports employee wellness. Below are some concepts that, when infused into supervisory settings, can promote recovery support as an organizational value.

- Prevention discussions are for every employee, not just those in recovery.
- The organization has a corporate commitment to wellness that is reflected in a resolution by its board of directors. (See "General Guidelines.")
- Prevention messages can be given by many different people, including first-line supervisors, upper management and EAP providers.
- Agency work is difficult and stressful. Working with the client population can result in vulnerability among staff members.
- The EAP is free to staff members and their families. It is confidential and can be used for any number of issues.
- Employees should think about their own support systems: Whom would they call on if problems occurred in their life? On whom can they rely for support?
- Ethics codes and codes of professional and personal conduct prohibit any substance use that impairs an employee's ability to do his or her job or that negatively affects the reputation or mission of the agency.
- The agency encourages employees to take responsibility and self-disclose substance abuse problems early before performance and behavior issues occur.

- Options such as medical leave may be applied in situations of misuse or relapse. In some circumstances, Federal rules, such as the Family Medical Leave Act, ensure job security.
- The organization's first and foremost responsibility is to its clients. Action should be taken to address employee use or misuse before any behavior rises to the level of misconduct that may jeopardize client health or safety.
- The organization believes at its core that people can change behavior and recover.

General Tips for Supervisory Conversations with Employees Suspected of Substance Misuse

Problems with the job behavior, workplace performance and ability to fulfill responsibilities can tip off a supervisor to the possibility that substance misuse is an issue for an employee. When broaching the subject with the employee, the supervisor should keep the following in mind:

- Focus on the work.
- Focus on what can be seen/observed (performance and behavior).
- Describe the behavior – what the employee did or said.
- Do not diagnose the employee.
- Do not be the employee's counselor or therapist.
- Do not make assumptions about why the behavior is occurring.
- Refer the employee to help if he or she might need it.
- Focus on topics that are legitimately part of the supervisory dialogue and do not discuss ones that are not.
- Remember that the supervisor's job is to improve performance.

Example

Ed has been working at Company XYZ for two years. He has been in the field for more than five years. He has always done average, not great, work. He is a counselor on the inpatient unit and has always talked openly about being in recovery. Over the past month, Ed has come in late three times. This morning, he came in an hour late without calling. Ed's supervisor has noticed that Ed looks disheveled lately. Normally clean-shaven and well-dressed, Ed has been coming into work without shaving and looking wrinkled. He also seems tired and run down. The supervisor is worried that Ed has relapsed.

It is legitimate and necessary for the supervisor to discuss Ed's tardiness with him. Unless the company has a clear policy about personal grooming or dress that Ed is violating, the supervisor probably should stay away from those topics.

Some guidelines for the discussion:

Have the conversation in private and focus on the behavior. "I've noticed that you've been late three times over the last few weeks, and rather than getting better on its own, this issue seems to be getting a little worse. Today, you were late and also didn't call in to let us know. I'm sure you realize that this violates the Hours of Work Policy. Can we agree that this behavior is going to improve? It causes some problems on the unit when you're late, especially when we can't plan for it and don't know if you're coming to work."

This approach – focusing on Ed's behavior – opens the door for Ed to let the supervisor know that something is going on to cause the tardiness and enables the supervisor to avoid saying directly that she is worried Ed may be relapsing, which might be more likely to get a defensive and resistant response.

During the course of the conversation, Ed tells the supervisor that his wife left him about six weeks ago. He is now a single parent of their 18-month-old daughter, who has been having trouble sleeping at night and getting up in the morning. In addition, Ed now bears the responsibility for taking his daughter to day care in the morning. He hasn't really wanted to talk about this situation because he was hoping it would get better and that his wife would come home. But she hasn't, and now he thinks they might be headed for divorce.

The supervisor offers to adjust Ed's hours for up to 30 days so that Ed can find a more convenient day care arrangement for his daughter. He can come in 30 minutes later and then take a shorter lunch or leave 30 minutes later. The supervisor also reminds Ed that the EAP would be a good place to get some help with issues related to his separation. The supervisor gives Ed an EAP brochure and tells him that he can take some time off work to attend an EAP appointment if needed. The supervisor hopes that if Ed goes to the EAP, a counselor will talk to him about whether his recovery support needs bolstering during this difficult time.

Managing Supervisory and Clinical Boundaries

Resisting the temptation to diagnose and provide counseling is one of the most difficult challenges for managers in the addictions field who face potential misuse among employees. Finding the proper balance of clinical knowledge and managerial strategy is critical to responding in a way that best serves the employee and limits liability for the employer.

Below are some examples of common mistakes that supervisors make when dealing with staff members who are having performance problems that might be related to a substance misuse issue. The circumstances underlying all of these examples are that the employee in question has had the following recent problems: absenteeism, low billing hours and a complaint from a client that telephone messages are not being returned.

Scenario #1: The Supervisor Says:

"You've been really irresponsible lately. I think you're having trouble with your recovery. I think you have relapsed. You need to take a drug test today."

Mistakes presented with this approach:

- *"I think you're having trouble with your recovery."* The supervisor identifies the employee as someone in recovery, implying that if he weren't in recovery the supervisor would not be requiring a drug test.
- *"I think you have relapsed."* The supervisor diagnoses the problem.
- *"You've been really irresponsible lately."* The supervisor uses general terms, rather than stating specifically what the problems are.

Scenario #2: The Supervisor Says:

"I've noticed lately that you've been tardy, your billings are down and one of your clients called complaining that you're not returning her calls. I think you may have relapsed. You need to take a drug test."

- *"You've been tardy, your billings are down and your client called complaining that you're not returning her calls."* The supervisor is much more specific about the job-related behavior that seems to be a problem.

- *"I think you may have relapsed."* The supervisor still diagnoses the problem and by using the term "relapsed," tacitly identifies the staff person as being in recovery.
- *"You need to take a drug test today."* The supervisor invokes an interventional response – a drug test – too early in the disciplinary process.

Scenario #3: The Supervisor Says:

"I am really concerned about some things that I have noticed about your work lately. You have been late five times in the last month. Your billings are down by 25% this month, and I just got a complaint from one of your clients that she has called you three times and you haven't returned her phone calls. These are important performance problems that need to improve. I am going to give you a written warning today and put you on a performance plan. At the very least, you need to be on time to work, you need to meet your billing goals and you need to respond to your clients. Is there anything you need from me to help you in these areas?

"I have noticed over the years that sometimes issues that are going on in an employee's personal life can negatively affect work performance. You know, of course, that our EAP program is available to you and your family. It's free and confidential. If there is something going on in your life outside of work that might be contributing to your performance problems, I want to really encourage you to give the EAP a call or use your own support network.

"Whatever you do to improve your performance, I want to be clear about my expectations: Over the next 30 days at a minimum, I expect that you will be on time, you will make your billing goal and you will respond to your clients. If you think of anything you need from me or anything I can do to help, let's be sure to talk about it."

- *"I am really concerned about some things that I have noticed about your work lately. You have been late five times in the last month. Your billings are down by 25% this month, and I just got a complaint from one of your clients that she has called you three times and you haven't returned her phone calls."* The supervisor is specific about performance issues and conveys immediate concern about those issues.

- *"I am going to give you a written warning today and put you on a performance plan."* The supervisor is specific about disciplinary consequences.
- *"At the very least, you need to be on time to work, you need to meet your billing goals and you need to respond to your clients."* The supervisor is specific about her expectations for performance improvement.
- *"Is there anything you need from me to help you in these areas?"* The supervisor opens the door for the employee to discuss any issues, free from judgment.
- *"I have noticed over the years that sometimes issues that are going on in an employee's personal life can negatively affect work performance. You know, of course, that our EAP program is available to you and your family. It's free and confidential. If there is something going on in your life outside of work that might be contributing to your performance problems, I want to really encourage you to give the EAP a call or use your own support network."* The supervisor encourages the employee to seek support without any implication about what may be wrong. The supervisor mentions the EAP in a general context of previous experience, taking the employee off the defensive.
- *"Whatever you do to improve your performance, I want to be clear about my expectations."* The supervisor's bottom line is the improvement of the employee's performance.

Access to Healthcare and Other Related Benefits: Guidelines for Employers

Establishing an Environment of Wellness

There are many policies and employee benefits that can help employers provide preventive services and intervene with employees who experience substance misuse problems. As noted throughout this toolkit, policies do not operate well in a vacuum. Many rely on the availability of other policies to create a seamless and effective response. It is helpful for employers to envision a set of related benefits. Whenever possible, benefits should be developed as a package that helps meet agency goals, including supporting employee wellness.

Financial challenges put constant pressure on agencies to limit their attempts to provide a robust set of benefits. In a challenging fiscal environment, viewing benefits as an interconnected set of tools for promoting wellness can lead to creative solutions. For example, strengthening EAP services or disability benefits may help fill gaps where a health insurance package falls short. Other options could include salary replacement to help employees pay for treatment that insurance doesn't cover or negotiating with an EAP to provide several sessions of services rather than just an assessment.

Health Insurance

Expenditures for employee health benefits are among the largest costs faced by organizations in the addictions field, often ranking second only to employee salaries. All indications are that health insurance costs will continue to rise. Additionally, some health insurance companies consider the addictions field a relatively risky business, potentially making insurance premiums even higher. These issues intensify the challenges facing agencies trying to provide strong employee benefits packages.

As discussed in Appendix A "Summary of Relevant Federal Laws," The Paul Wellstone and Pete Domenici Mental Health Parity and Addiction Equity Act of 2008 was signed into law on October 3, 2008, as part of the $700 billion financial rescue package. The measure requires companies providing health insurance to cover mental health and addiction on the same basis as physical conditions. These provisions will go into effect one year after their enactment (October 8, 2009). The mental health and addictions provisions:

- Apply to group health plans with 51 or more members
- Forbid employers and insurers from placing stricter limits on mental healthcare than on other health conditions
- Apply to out-of-network coverage, so that plans providing network coverage must also provide such coverage for mental health conditions
- Leave in place any existing state parity measures
- Require that the US Department of Labor, US Department of Health and Human Services and the Treasury Department issue regulations by October 2009

Once the Act and its provisions are enacted, insurance benefits for substance abuse and mental health treatment may increase for many workers in the addictions field. Until that time, or for those with group plans with fewer than 51 members, the guidelines in this section may be helpful.

In the context of use, misuse and wellness, where do these pressures leave agencies trying to provide access to addictions treatment services as part of a set of workplace policies? In general, employers covering more than 100 employees have more flexibility in providing robust benefits because they can ask insurers to customize benefit plans. For example, these employers can ask insurance companies bidding on their business to provide quotes for plans that include enriched benefits for substance abuse and mental health services. Many organizations fear asking for these enriched benefits because of what the additions might do to premiums; however, increased coverage for outpatient treatment and mental health services usually does not increase premiums dramatically (sometimes even less than 1%). Because outpatient services tend to be cost-effective, enriching the insurance benefits for these services can be a meaningful and cost-effective addition to an employer's set of responses to substance use problems among its employees. It should be noted here that health maintenance organization (HMO) plans are usually filed with the State and therefore cannot be amended or customized. Preferred provider organization (PPO) plans and point of service (POS) plans, however, are generally more easily customized.

Larger plans also can be more flexible in offering benefits to part-time employees. To mitigate the additional premium costs of adding these employees to plans, employers can increase the premium co-pay for these employees, thus allowing them to participate in the plan but at a greater cost.

Because larger organizations have greater purchasing power, smaller organizations may consider entering a consortium of similar organizations to bolster their purchasing power with insurers. Generally speaking, this is not an advisable solution. Such consortiums are often cumbersome and difficult to manage, particularly for agencies with limited human resources staff. In addition, because insurers tend to place addictions treatment providers in a riskier pool, assembling multiple providers into one purchasing consortium may exacerbate risk and actually increase costs.

Although not advisable for health benefits, joint purchasing can be an effective strategy for negotiating with and purchasing EAP services. To the extent that employers supplement health insurance with EAP offerings, they can maintain a wellness environment that supports a wide range of personal workforce concerns and issues.

Impaired Professionals Programs

Impaired professionals programs (IPP) have emerged around the country as important resources for individuals seeking to return to work and preserve their required certification or licensure while maintaining accountability for following a treatment plan. IPP configurations vary from State to State and from industry to industry. The basic structure includes an agreement between the professional and the IPP whereby the IPP makes an independent referral to treatment according to the particular circumstances, monitors the individual's progress and, based on the individual's progress or lack thereof, decides if he or she should maintain certification or licensure and continue to practice.

Impaired professionals programs are popular in industries where professionals have medical, fiduciary or safety responsibilities to clients – for example, doctors, nurses, lawyers, pilots, etc. At present, IPPs are not widespread in the addictions treatment field. It is beyond the purview of this toolkit to discuss establishment of an IPP; however, it must be noted that IPPs can be valuable independent resources for a field like addictions treatment where employees may be at increased risk for use, misuse and relapse.

See Also: Employee Assistance Program; Summary of Relevant Federal Laws

III. ORGANIZATIONAL POLICIES

> Please Note: The resources, tools and other information presented in this toolkit are offered as guidance for treatment provider agencies use. They are designed to be as universally applicable as possible. While every attempt has been made to ensure they meet legal requirements, they should not be substituted for independent legal counsel. Additional local, State and Federal laws may apply.

Code of Professional Conduct

A Code of Professional Conduct presents the underlying principles of organizational operations and expectations for employee behavior related to those principles.

A clearly written and enforced Code of Professional Conduct can be an effective tool for the prevention of workplace use and misuse. It defines a set of behaviors that are unacceptable and subject to disciplinary action.

Components of a Retention-Oriented Code of Professional Conduct

Organizations can use the components described below to develop, add to or enhance their existing policies.

Prevention

Codes of Professional Conduct in the addictions field are often grounded in several key principles. Violation of any of these principles may prompt disciplinary action and/or intervention. The underlying principles include:

- Non-discrimination
- Client welfare
- Client and professional relationships
- Compliance with rules and laws
- Preventing harm
- Duty of care

Policy in Practice

A Code of Professional Conduct clearly prohibits any behavior that compromises an employee's ability to accomplish his or her job responsibilities or the reputation of the agency. This prohibition necessarily includes substance use and misuse. Many of the behaviors prohibited by the code could be warning signs of substance misuse. Some of these behaviors are discussed in more detail in "Red Flags That Staff May Be Misusing Substances." Because the Code of Professional Conduct covers a range of behaviors, it should prompt a range of managerial responses, including increased monitoring, drug testing, an EAP referral, and disciplinary action up to and including termination.

A Code of Professional Conduct need not be limited to on-the-job behavior. It also allows the agency to be concerned with off-duty behavior *when the behavior jeopardizes the agency's mission or reputation* and employee performance. Off-duty inappropriate behavior, including substance misuse- related behavior that occurs during off-duty hours (as it often does), may open the door for intervention,.

While it is common practice for organizations and licensing and certifying bodies to have Codes of Professional Conduct signed by employees or licensees, it is not a common practice for these policies to be used in managerial settings. A Code of Professional Conduct can be used as a managerial tool, whether as part of a regular performance review process or when intervening with staff members who may be, or suspected to be, using substances. Managers can use the code to help employees identify areas where there are compliance issues. For example, a manager might say, "You agreed under the Code of Professional Conduct to avoid bringing personal or professional issues into the counseling relationship. Why is that important? Do you feel you're in a position to do that?"

SAMPLE POLICY

Professional ethics are the core of addictions treatment work. Although the Code of Professional Conduct offers a set of principles to help guide decision-making when ethical issues arise, it does not provide a set of rules prescribing how staff should act in all situations.

Principle 1: Non-Discrimination

- I must not discriminate against clients or professionals based on religion, race, age, sex, disability, national ancestry, sexual orientation or economic condition.

Principle 2: Legal and Moral Standards

- I must protect the welfare and dignity of the client and respect the laws of the communities where they work. Violations of legal standards may damage both my reputation and the agency's.
- I will not physically, verbally, emotionally or sexually abuse clients.
- I will not abuse alcohol or other legal drugs.
- I will not possess or use any illegal drugs.
- I must honestly represent my qualifications, educational background and professional credentials.
- I will not aid or abet a person to misrepresent his/her professional qualifications.

Principle 3: Competence

- I will provide professional services only within the boundaries of my competence based on education, training and experience.
- I will pursue professional development by taking advantage of continuing education and other opportunities for professional development to maintain a high level of competence.

Principle 4: Client Relationships

- I will not enter into professional helping relationships with members of client families and client friends, with people closely connected to clients or members of their families, or with others whose welfare might be jeopardized by such a dual role.
- I will not engage in romantic or sexual relationships with current clients, former clients, or clients' families or close associates. I will not engage in romantic or sexual relationships with clients for at least one year following termination of treatment.
- I will refrain from socializing with clients and clients' family members or close associates.
- I will not use derogatory language to or about clients. I will use respectful language in all communications to and about clients.

Principle 5: Confidentiality

- I will comply with all Federal, State and local laws, rules and regulations pertaining to client confidentiality.
- I will guard professional confidences and reveal them only in compliance with the law or when there is clear and imminent danger to an individual or society, and then only to appropriate professionals and responsible authorities. Confidential information can be revealed when doing so is in the best interest of a client or the welfare of others, or when obligations to society or legal requirements demand revelation.
- I will discuss information revealed in a clinical or professional setting only in appropriate settings and only for professional purposes clearly concerned with a case.

- I understand that information and materials used in teaching and training must not identify clients.

Principle 6: Professional Relationships

- I will not knowingly withhold information from colleagues and other professionals if the information has been properly released and will enhance client care.
- When working in a treatment team, I will not abdicate my responsibility to protect and promote the welfare and best interests of the client.
- I will not exploit clients in disputes with other colleagues or engage clients in any inappropriate discussions of conflicts between them and their colleagues. These colleagues include those in my own agency and staff from allied agencies.

Principle 7: Conflicts of Interest

- I will be alert to and avoid conflicts of interest that interfere with the exercise of professional discretion and judgment.
- I will refrain from entering into any formal or informal activity or agreement that presents a conflict of interest or is inconsistent with the conscientious performance of duties.
- I will refrain from allowing personal interest to impair my objectivity in the performance of duty.

Principle 8: Remuneration

- I will not charge private fees to clients.
- I must not use relationships with clients for personal or professional gain or the profit of any agency or commercial enterprise. I must not engage in any economic relationship with any client.
- I will not give or receive any kind of fee, commission, rebate or any other form of compensation for the referral of clients.

> **Principle 9: Ethical Violations**
>
> - In circumstances where I am aware of ethical violations or potential ethical violations, it is my obligation to attempt to rectify the situation. In instances in which an intervention fails, I will report the failure to my supervisor or other management staff.
> - Management will investigate incidents and circumstances in which the Code of Professional Conduct may have been violated. Based on investigation findings, disciplinary action up to and including termination may be taken.

It is also important that a Code of Professional Conduct be made a topic of regular discussion and training. Workers new to the field and workers coming from other fields may be unfamiliar with ethics codes and need to be coached on their importance.

See Also: Red Flags That Staff May Be Using Substances; Drug Testing

Disclaimer: This policy should not substitute for independent legal review of local, State and Federal laws applicable to your agency. Consult an attorney prior to the implementation of any new organizational policy.

Drug-Free Workplace Policy

A Drug-Free Workplace Policy is a definitive statement that any and all activity related to drug or alcohol use or sale is prohibited. Federal contractors and grantees that receive Federal contracts of more than $100,000 are required to have a Drug-Free Workplace Policy. Merely having a policy, however, does not make an employer compliant. For more information, see "Guide to Relevant Federal Laws."

A Drug-Free Workplace Policy has both prevention and intervention roles. This policy is likely to be the single strongest statement an agency can make about prohibition of drug use by employees on the job or, potentially, outside the workplace. The policy encourages access to an EAP and insists on compliance as a term of employment.

Components of a Retention-Oriented Drug-Free Workplace Policy

Organizations can use the components described below to develop, add to or enhance their existing policies.

Prevention

Organizations can use the following Drug-Free Workplace policy components to prevent substance use and misuse:

- Blanket prohibition of drug or alcohol use in the work setting
- Restrictions against reporting to work under the influence
- Discretion to take disciplinary action related to drug and alcohol use outside the workplace to the extent that these behaviors may affect job performance

Intervention

The following policy components define how Drug-Free Workplace may be used as an intervention tool.

- Discretion concerning the response employed
- Leveraging compliance as a requirement of further employment
- Encouragement to use the EAP

Policy in Practice

A Drug-Free Workplace Policy is meant to be a clear statement by the agency that drug and alcohol use, possession, sale, manufacture, dispensation, etc., are strictly prohibited at the work site at any site where the employee might conduct work and at any time the employee is doing the work of the agency. This strict prohibition accomplishes the policy's preventative function.

A Drug-Free Workplace Policy can further prohibit these activities *outside of work hours* to the extent that the agency regards use or misuse as either impairing the employee's ability to do his or her job or threatening the reputation and mission of the agency. The phrase "to the extent the agency regards" is central to the scope and effectiveness of this policy, particularly because the policy includes alcohol, which is legal. Without this invocation of organizational discretion, the policy could be read as a prohibition of the use of all drugs *including alcohol* by employees during non-work hours. Including this provision allows the agency to determine whether off-duty behavior merits intervention and/or discipline.

SAMPLE POLICY

[*AGENCY*] adheres to the requirements of the Drug-Free Workplace Act of 1988. Use of controlled substances subjects coworkers, colleagues, funding sources, clients, visitors and others to unacceptable and needless safety risks and undermines the agency's mission and operating effectiveness.

Reporting to work or working under the influence of a controlled substance or alcohol is strictly prohibited. Exceptions will be made for prescribed medications; however, misuse of prescribed medications leading to impairment is similarly prohibited. This prohibition extends to agency premises and to all other sites where employees may engage in agency business.

[*AGENCY*] prohibits the criminal use, manufacture, distribution, dispensation, possession, or sale of a controlled substance or alcohol at any affiliated worksite. Such conduct is prohibited outside scheduled working hours to the extent that [*AGENCY*] regards the behavior as impairing the employee's ability to perform on the job or as threatening to the reputation and mission of the agency.

Employees who are convicted of a violation related to a controlled substance or alcohol (or who plead no contest to such a charge), must notify the human resources department in writing within five working days of the conviction or plea.

If you would like information on locally available sources of substance use or alcohol-related counseling, [*AGENCY*] sponsors an EAP, which is available to all employees and their families.

Violation of this policy may result in disciplinary action up to and including termination. [*AGENCY*] may also require that an employee successfully complete a substance use or rehabilitation program as a condition of further employment.

A Drug-Free Workplace Policy can also incorporate managerial discretion regarding interventions that occur as a result of policy violation(s). By not prescribing specific responses, the policy allows the agency a wide range of responses based on individual circumstances. The agency can refer to the

EAP, discipline the employee, recommend leave or treatment, or terminate an employee based on a violation. Since managerial discretion is built into the policy, agency management needs to be careful to ensure that similarly situated employees are treated equitably.

See Also: Summary of Relevant Federal Laws

Disclaimer: This policy should not substitute for independent legal review of local, State and Federal laws applicable to your agency. Consult an attorney prior to the implementation of any new organizational policy.

Drug Testing Policy

Drug testing is a tool by which employers can confirm or refute suspected substance use by an employee. When used as part of a clearly defined process, drug testing also can serve a preventive role by putting employees on notice that they can and will be tested in certain situations. That knowledge alone may discourage use.

Components of a Retention-Oriented Drug Testing Policy
Organizations can use the components described below to develop, add to or enhance their existing policies.

Prevention
The following policy component can be used by organizations to reveal warning signs of possible substance use and trigger a proactive response:

- Pre-employment testing after a conditional offer of employment

Intervention
The following policy components define how drug testing may be used as an intervention tool.

- Reasonable-cause testing at the discretion of the supervisor

Re- Entry
The following policy component allows the organization to continue to monitor the employee's situation while supporting treatment.

- Incorporation of testing as part of any return-to-work plan or contract

Policy in Practice

Pre-employment Testing. The Americans with Disabilities Act (ADA) bans discrimination based on recovery status, but does not protect employees or candidates for employment who are currently using illegal drugs. Many employers assume that ADA regulations preclude them from requiring a pre-employment drug test. In fact, the ADA prohibits pre–offer medical tests; however, the law makes a distinction between testing for illegal drugs, which is not considered a medical test, and testing for alcohol which is considered a medical test.

Job candidates can be required to provide a drug test before employment at any point during the hiring process. To comply with the ADA, however, tests for alcohol should be administered only after a conditional offer of employment has been made and accepted. In practice, it may be easier to administer pre- employment drug or alcohol tests after an offer has been made or accepted.

Reasonable Cause Testing. Agencies can have a policy that allows for testing for reasonable cause. Under such a policy, if a manager believes there is reasonable cause to suspect drug use, he or she can require a drug test. The policy may also allow for termination upon refusal to provide a specimen for testing. Examples of reasonable cause behaviors include those described in "Red Flags That Staff May Be Using Substances."

After a Positive Test. If an employee tests positive, he or she should be offered leave. Upon returning to work, the employee should be required to pass a drug test and to sign a return-to-work contract that requires random testing for a specified period of time (up to one year is recommended). A positive drug test while on such a contract would be grounds for termination.

A Word about Random Drug Testing
Some employers choose to or are required to implement a random drug-testing policy. Because these policies are expensive and require the advice of legal counsel, a sample policy is not included in this toolkit. Random drug testing policies can cast a "wide net"; consequently, the agency should give careful consideration to implementing such a policy. For example, the agency should have a plan for what to do when an employee tests positive but has no

work- related performance or behavior issues. The agency also must decide if it will test for alcohol and, if so, what happens if an employee tests positive. The employer must also decide about what to do when an employee tests positive for a prescription medication and the employee is able to produce the prescription. Despite these considerations, random drug testing does have advantages, one of which is the potential ability to intervene with an employee who may be misusing but has not yet experienced significant consequences of use.

SAMPLE POLICY

[*AGENCY'S*] drug testing program has been established to:

- Create and maintain a safe, healthy and efficient work environment for employees and clients
- Maintain agency credibility and the trust of constituents
- Help employees suffering from chemical dependency to successfully deal with the problem before it injures them, their careers, their dependents or the agency.

The program applies to all prospective employees and current employees.

Pre-Employment Testing

Procedures
[NOTE: This section should be edited to reflect the testing methodology your agency uses, including any testing conducted for prescription medication in addition to illicit substances.]

All applicants for employment will be required to sign a consent form agreeing to provide a urine specimen that will be tested for the presence of illegal drugs, and to submit to a Breathalyzer test for the presence of alcohol.

Any applicant to whom an offer of employment is extended and accepted will be required to produce a urine sample to be tested for the presence of controlled substances and may be subjected to a Breathalyzer test.

Pre-employment screening is required for all positions except for temporary staff obtained through an outside service. Part-time employees and temporary employees on the agency payroll must be tested.

Applicants are required to provide a specimen to the hiring authority within two days of the request. All pre-employment drug testing will be conducted by [ENTITY CONDUCTING THE TESTING] and will be protected by the standard chain of custody procedures. Screening results will be available within 48 hours of receipt of the test.

Employment may not commence unless and until negative results have been obtained.

Actions

Any applicant who refuses to sign the consent or to submit to a drug screening or Breathalyzer test will be denied further consideration for employment on the basis of the refusal.

Positive pre-employment tests will automatically be submitted for confirmation retest. Receipt of confirmation results may take up to 10 days, even for false positives. Employment may not commence unless and until negative test results have been obtained.

Any applicant who tests positive and confirms positive for illicit or illegal drug use (except as supported by active prescription) or tests positive for the presence of alcohol will be denied further consideration for employment and will not be reconsidered for employment for a period of one year following the positive test. Confirmation results will be the deciding factor, despite an applicant's claims to the contrary.

Employee Testing

Procedures

The need to test an employee will be based on reasonable suspicion resulting from but not limited to:

- Observable behaviors, such as the display of physical symptoms or manifestations of being under the influence of an illicit drug, prescription medications or alcohol
- Abnormal conduct or erratic behavior while at work, absenteeism, tardiness or deterioration in work performance

- Report of drug or alcohol use provided by reliable and credible sources

Requests for urine or Breathalyzer testing based on reasonable suspicion must be documented by the manager and authorized by the manager's supervisor, the human resources director or an executive staff member.

Actions

All positive test results will be automatically submitted for confirmation testing.

If a test result is positive, the employee may be mandated to the EAP for an evaluation. It will be at the manager's discretion whether or not subsequent positive tests result in EAP referrals or disciplinary actions.

Employees who test positive during their orientation period or while on probation are subject to immediate discharge.

Employees who test positive will be required to sign a contract agreeing to abstinence and to submit to random testing twice per month for a two-month period and monthly thereafter for up to 60 months.

Employment may be terminated for:

- Continued or resumed use as verified through testing
- Refusal or failure to attend the EAP evaluation
- Refusal to submit to testing as required above
- Refusal to sign the abstinence contract

Employee Protection

Specimen collection and testing under this policy will be performed in accordance with the following procedures:

- Dissemination of testing and results information will be limited to the employee, his or her superiors and the human resources department.
- Collection of specimens will be performed under reasonable and sanitary conditions. Individual dignity will be preserved to the extent practicable.

- Specimens will be collected in a manner reasonably calculated to prevent substitution of specimens and interference with collection or testing.

The employee will have the opportunity to provide any information he or she considers relevant, including identification of current or recently used prescription or non-prescription drugs or other relevant medical information, within three working days of notification of a confirmed positive result.

Testing for drugs or alcohol will comport to scientifically accepted analytical methods and procedures.

Every urine specimen that produces a positive confirmed result will be preserved for a period of 30 days from the time the results are delivered. During this period, the employee who provided the specimen will be permitted to have a portion of the specimen retested, at his or her expense, at a licensed laboratory chosen by the employee.

*[AGENCY] has invested in an Employee Assistance Program (EAP) as part of our commitment to help employees in a professional and confidential manner. While employees are always encouraged to use the EAP, doing so does not mitigate the application of disciplinary measures under any circumstances. They are parallel courses of action.

Refusal to Submit to a Drug Test. If a drug test is required or requested under any of the above circumstances and the employee fails to submit to the test, he or she is subject to immediate termination. Similarly, any evidence of tampering or adulterating a drug sample is grounds for immediate termination.

See Also: Employee Assistance Program; Return-to-Work Reintegration; Red Flags That Staff May Be Using Substances

Disclaimer: This policy should not substitute for independent legal review of local, State and Federal laws applicable to your agency. Consult an attorney prior to the implementation of any new organizational policy.

Paid Time off Policy

Paid Time Off (PTO) is a combined category under which an employee is paid for pre-approved time off. It is a fairly common practice for employers to offer several different types of paid time off, including sick time, vacation time, personal time, "floating" holidays, etc., and to manage each type separately. Today, however, the trend is toward simplifying the process by offering one or two types of paid time off, usually sick time and a more general paid time off that encompasses all other benefit time.

Like sick time, general PTO can be an important tool in supporting workplace retention. PTO abuses can be an indicator of substance use or the presence of stressors that may lead to relapse, and PTO can be leveraged to allow employees the opportunity to seek treatment and other support services.

Components of a Retention-Oriented Paid Time Off Policy

Organizations can use the components described below to develop, add to or enhance their existing policies.

Prevention

Organizations can use the following policy component to prevent unexpected absences:

- Pre-approval of PTO by a supervisor is required in advance of the day the time is to be taken.

Intervention

The following policy component allows the use of PTO for treatment or recovery support purposes:

- Employees can use PTO to attend treatment or other support services.

Re- Entry

The following policy components allow an organization to support an employee's re-entry to work while he or she continues to participate in treatment or recovery support services:

- Employees can use PTO to supplement modified or reduced work schedules while seeking treatment or recovery support (subject to approval and other applicable policies).

Policy in Practice

Unplanned, unauthorized or excessive use of PTO can be a warning sign of substance misuse. To leverage the value of PTO, the policy should be written to require prior notification and supervisory authorization.

SAMPLE POLICY

[*AGENCY*] provides paid time off (PTO) for regular full-time and eligible part-time employees. Paid time off is to be used for rest and recreation and to attend to personal business, religious observances and other matters important to you. Paid time off earnings depend on length of service as follows:

[*Insert appropriate terms and conditions appropriate here.*]

We encourage you to use your PTO during the year in which it is earned. Unused PTO will be carried over into the next year; however, at no time may an employee accrue PTO in excess of [*Insert appropriate terms here.*]

Requests to use PTO must be submitted in writing to your immediate supervisor no less than two weeks in advance. Approval of your time-off request is subject to the needs of your unit as determined by your supervisor.

You may use only PTO that you have already earned. You may not take extra time off in anticipation of future earnings. PTO balances will not be paid in lieu of time off except upon termination of employment. You may not use PTO in lieu of your final day worked.

If the company so chooses, PTO can be used to provide salary replacement while an employee seeks treatment or other supportive services, whether or not the employee takes a leave of absence. Similarly, PTO can be used following leave, allowing the employee to work part time and use PTO to make up some of the difference between the hours worked and full salary. It is not advisable to allow employees to use benefit time such as PTO or sick time to make up the difference between hours worked and 100% of salary. Doing so can provide a disincentive to return to work full time and also may also create a negative ripple effect among other employees who are working their full-time hours and perhaps additional hours to cover the responsibilities of the employee in question.

See Also: Sick Time; Return-to-Work Reintegration

Disclaimer: This policy should not substitute for independent legal review of local, State and Federal laws applicable to your agency. Consult an attorney prior to the implementation of any new organizational policy.

Sick Time Policy

Sick time is a form of paid time off applied when an employee has a medical need, such as being sick or having a doctor's appointment. Sick time applies to situations in which work is missed in hours or a minimal number of days. It covers all medical-related situations short of a formal leave policy.

Sick time also supports workplace retention efforts. Abuse of sick time may be an indicator of substance use or the presence of stressors that may lead to relapse. In addition, sick time can give employees the opportunity to seek treatment and other support services and promote overall wellness.

Components of a Retention-Oriented Sick Time Policy
Organizations can use the components described below to develop, add to or enhance their existing policies.

Prevention
Organizations can use the following policy components as warning signs of possible substance use and as triggers for a proactive response:

- After a specified number of absences in a fixed time (for example, three days in a row or, five days in a one month), a doctor's note is mandatory.
- Unapproved absences the day after a holiday and vacation extension require a doctor's note
- Sick time that requires a doctor's note will remain unpaid until the note is produced. If no note is produced within a certain time frame, the pay docking will be permanent and other responses may take effect (for example, mandatory EAP referral).

Intervention

The following policy components allow the use of sick time for treatment or recovery support purposes. Employees can:

- Use sick time to attend treatment
- Modify or reduce work schedules while seeking treatment or recovery support (subject to approval and other applicable policies)
- Use sick time to attend EAP sessions
- Use sick time to travel to another community for treatment or EAP and self-help groups, which is particularly useful when the agency is in a smaller community.

Re-Entry

The following policy components allow the organization to continue to monitor the employee's situation while supporting treatment.

- Employees can use sick time to come back to work on a modified schedule (subject to approval and other applicable policies).
- Returning employees must submit to a drug test.

Policy in Practice

Because sick time is a potential indicator of substance use, companies can take steps to ensure that sick time is used for legitimate illnesses and that reasonable maximums are in place. For example, a supervisor can talk directly to an employee who calls in with an unplanned absence, which allows the supervisor to listen for indications of impairment (slurred speech, disorientation, etc.). This contact also allows the supervisor to tell the employee if a medical note (or other documentation) is required for the absence to be authorized.

SAMPLE POLICY

If you are a regular full-time or eligible part-time employee, [AGENCY] provides you with sick days to use when you are unable to work due to non-work-related illness or injury. On the first day of the month following six months of employment, you will begin to earn 5.625 hours of sick time per month (9 days per year), up to a maximum of 337.5 hours (45 days).

Sick time is charged in quarter-hour increments. Sick time may be carried over from year to year, but once you reach the maximum, no additional sick time will be earned until the balance is reduced.

In order for absences due to non-work related illness or injury to be authorized, [AGENCY] has the right, at any time, to require that you obtain a statement from your doctor. This statement should confirm that you are (or were) medically unable to work, outline the duration (or expected) duration of your illness, and state when you are likely to be able to return to work. [AGENCY] does not seek information regarding your medical diagnosis. A physician's note is required in the following instances:

- After three consecutive days of sick time used
- After five days of sick time used in a one-month period
- For use of sick time immediately preceding or following other paid time off such as a holiday
- In any other circumstances in which your supervisor deems it necessary

In the instances outlined above, a medical note must be submitted to your supervisor and included with your time sheet for that period. Failure to provide such medical documentation will cause the absence to be considered unauthorized and may result in disciplinary action including, but not limited to, wage reduction, written warning, suspension and termination.

Sick time will not be paid in lieu of time taken nor will it be paid out at termination of employment. You may not use sick time in lieu of final day worked.

Medical, dental, mental health, addictions and other counseling or treatment appointments may be charged against your sick time, as may travel to those appointments if local services are not available.

Sick time may be used to offset modified work schedules as a result of a medical issue. This use must be approved in advance in writing by your supervisor and the human resources department.

Additionally, policies for "calling in" can require that the employee speak directly to his or her supervisor, to a human resources person or to another supervisor or manager designated to take these calls in the supervisor's absence. The employee also can be required to call during a certain period of time (such as within 30 minutes of scheduled start time) and to talk to a live person – that is, no voice mail, email or texting.

As a tool for supporting employee wellness, companies can encourage employee use of sick time for appropriate purposes, thus creating an environment where sick time can be used to access treatment and recovery support services. To maintain the integrity of this role, companies should separate sick time from other PTO policies thereby allowing staff to have a bank of sick time separate from personal days or holidays. Companies also can offer enough sick time to cover any potential treatment regimen and allow sick time to be spent in hours as well as days. To promote the use of sick time for these purposes, companies should not encourage employees to bank sick time as bonus days off or as payouts of unused time at termination (unless required to do so by law).

See Also: Corporate Commitment to Employee Wellness; Paid Time Off; Employee Assistance Program; Return-to-Work Reintegration

Disclaimer: This policy should not substitute for independent legal review of local, State and Federal laws applicable to your agency. Consult an attorney prior to the implementation of any new organizational policy.

Hours of Work Policy

An Hours of Work Policy outlines when employees are expected to perform their job functions. Lack of accountability for time throughout the workday is a common problem for employees experiencing substance misuse. Violations of the Hours of Work Policy can be used as indicators that an employee may be having a problem.

Components of a Retention-Oriented Hours of Work Policy
Organizations can use the components described below to develop, add to or enhance their existing policies.

Prevention
When added to an Hours of Work Policy, the following components help ensure that employees follow the schedule defined for them and provide a framework for preventing employee problems:

- Specific start and end times for the work day as well as specific break and lunch times
- Requirement that variances from the regular work schedule must be approved by a supervisor
- Statement that travel time to work is part of the employee's normal commute and is not included in work time.

SAMPLE POLICY

[*AGENCY's*] regular work week is [*insert details*] hours, or [*X*] hours per day. The core business hours for the agency are [*insert details*], Monday through Friday. Your particular schedule will depend on the needs of your department as determined by your department head.

If you work a(n) [*X*]-hour day, you are entitled to take a one-hour unpaid lunch break between [*insert details*] and a 15-minute break each morning and each afternoon. Your lunch hour and breaks should be coordinated with your supervisor to ensure adequate office coverage.

Executive staff may adjust weekly schedules from time to time to meet changing needs.

Your pay is based on your hours on the job, including breaks but excluding lunch hours. You may not work more than [X] hours in any one work week without your supervisor's prior written approval. You also must have approval for any agency work done away from your customary workplace.

Travel time to and from your regularly assigned workplace is considered commuting, not hours worked, and is not compensable.

Policy in Practice

Supervisors should be vigilant about their employees' hours of work. Lack of accountability for being on time can be an indicator that an employee may have issues in his or her life causing either a logistical or psychological distraction resulting in the inability to meet scheduled work times. An Hours of Work Policy allows the supervisor to legitimately intervene based on the behavior as a workplace issue. Common hours of work problems include:

- Long lunches
- Extended breaks

- Work time that is unaccounted for
- Extended time "in the field" that is unaccounted for

These and other observable issues are discussed in more detail in "Red Flags That an Employee May Be Using Substances." When these issues arise, supervisors should note them and view them as possible indicators of a substance misuse problem, especially if they occur while other performance and behavior problems are present.

See Also: Red Flags That Staff May Be Using Substances

Disclaimer: This policy should not substitute for independent legal review of local, State and Federal laws applicable to your agency. Consult an attorney prior to the implementation of any new organizational policy.

Employee Assistance Program

An Employee Assistance Program (EAP) provides a confidential assessment and referral source designed to help employees and their family members address a myriad of challenging issues, such as legal matters, finances, mental health, marriage, family, other relationship concerns, addiction, work-related problems and stress. Typically, the EAP is administered by a neutral third party contracted by the employer. While the employer may refer an employee to the EAP, actual EAP use is confidential. In most cases, the EAP is only a referral source – employees pay for the services they use but may qualify for reimbursement or coverage under the agency's health insurance plan.

An EAP can be a critical partner in helping the agency deal with issues of use and misuse in the workplace. By sponsoring the EAP, the agency is telling employees it values staff well-being and that employees have immediate access to confidential services. The EAP helps mitigate reservations supervisors may have about overstepping supervisory and clinical boundaries. The supervisor can make a referral to the EAP, thus facilitating access to services without needing to know any of the specific details.

How to Find a High-Quality EAP
The Employee Assistance Professionals Association (EAPAA) can help an agency find an EAP. EAPAA's Web site, www.eapassn.org, features an

EAP Buyer's Guide designed to help employers know what to look for when seeking an EAP.

Components of a Retention-Oriented EAP Policy

Organizations can use the components described below to develop, add to or enhance their existing policies.

Intervention

The EAP is inherently an intervention program. An organization can use the following components to enhance its effectiveness:

- Agency subsidization of more than just the initial EAP assessment
- Ability for both self-referrals and supervisor-mandated referrals
- Services available to family members
- Parallel application of EAP referrals and disciplinary guidelines
- Availability of EAP services for terminated employees for a fixed period of time

Re-Entry

The following policy component allows the organization to continue to monitor the employee's situation while supporting treatment.

- Mandatory EAP participation as part of a return-to-work program or contract

Policy in Practice

Whenever possible, agencies should have an EAP program. Smaller agencies that may not have the funds to contract with an EAP provider may be able to pool resources with other smaller agencies or, at the very least, can have a list of community resources available that employees can access.

The EAP's goal is to help employees effectively deal with any personal problems that may be contributing to problems at work. The employer's goal is to help employees improve their performance without directly treating the underlying causes of performance issues. To improve performance employers can use tools like formal discipline, training, re-training and modifying responsibilities, increasing supervision, and referral to the EAP.

Often, the EAP Policy is used most effectively in combination with a policy of progressive discipline, as well as Drug Testing, Employee Leave and

Return to Work policies. It is important for managers and supervisors to understand how these policies work together.

Services Provided by the EAP: Whenever possible, EAP services should include several sessions with the EAP provider – not just an assessment and referral. Employers should keep this in mind when negotiating with EAP providers.

Use of the EAP: The EAP can be a valuable tool for improving employee job performance when performance is affected by personal issues including, but not limited to, substance misuse. An EAP Policy should allow for both self- referral and supervisory referral. When a supervisor makes a mandatory referral the supervisor has the right to know whether the employee shows up for the meeting. However, information regarding the EAP session is confidential.

Availability of Services to Family Members: Whenever possible, EAP services should be made available to all members of the employee's family. Often, when a family member is having problems, the employee may exhibit job performance issues. Additionally, an employee's family members can use the EAP as a resource, particularly in cases of relapse, without employer involvement. As a result, EAP services should be widely and frequently advertised to employees and their families.

Confidentiality: EAPs must provide services on a confidential basis. Employees need to trust that if they voluntarily go to the EAP, the use of the service and the content of sessions are strictly confidential. Exceptions to the confidentiality rule may apply if a supervisor makes a mandatory referral to the EAP or if employee attendance at the EAP is made a condition of returning to work after a leave due to a substance abuse issue. In these instances, only the fact of the employee's attendance at the session(s) can be disclosed to the employer without the written consent of the employee.

Although the policy allows the EAP to disclose meeting content to the employer with the employee's written consent, it is recommended that employers use caution when asking for information regarding the content of EAP or other treatment meetings. The more the employer knows about issues the client is dealing with in treatment, the easier it is for supervisors and other managers to cross the line between employer and therapist. The recommended role for supervisors and managers is to make the referral, encourage attendance, monitor job performance and provide appropriate management to improve job performance.

It is not unusual, especially in smaller communities, for professionals in the addictions field to know local EAP providers. Employers should be aware of potential problems of familiarity. Employees are less likely to avail themselves of EAP services if they know the counselors personally. Whenever necessary and possible, employees should be offered opportunities to access services in another community in order to avoid these situations. Employers should discuss this possibility with EAP providers during contract negotiations. One of the key issues in negotiations should be the EAP's flexibility, either in broadening its provider network or in allowing services to be provided outside of the network when necessary.

Use of the EAP during Disciplinary Processes: Many managers are uncomfortable mandating EAP participation or combining an EAP referral with disciplinary processes. The effective combination of these strategies, however, is critical. Employers should consider an EAP referral (even when it is mandated) as a process that runs parallel to ongoing disciplinary processes, as opposed to being part of the disciplinary process itself.

SAMPLE POLICY

[*AGENCY*] sponsors an Employee Assistance Program (EAP), which is available to all employees and their families. The EAP is there to assist you in times when the challenges of life make it difficult to cope.

What Is an Employee Assistance Program?

The EAP is a confidential assessment and referral source ready to help you or your family members address legal issues, finances, mental health, marriage, family, other relationship concerns, addiction, work-related problems, stress or anything else that may be troubling you.

The EAP is administered by a neutral third party with whom [*AGENCY*] contracts to provide EAP services. Your contact with the EAP is confidential; the agency never knows who self-refers or what particular issues are addressed.

Our arrangement with the EAP provides for an initial assessment; if you choose to follow the EAP-recommended treatment or course of action, subsequent charges will be your responsibility or may be submitted for payment under your health insurance plan if the service is covered. The EAP will attempt to make recommendations that work within your means.

Self-Referral

To access the EAP, simply call the EAP administrator listed below: [number(s) for different offices]

Supervisory Referral

Your supervisor may mandate an EAP assessment. If your issues begin to affect your job performance or attendance, your supervisor may refer you to the EAP in an attempt to improve your workplace performance and enhance your overall wellness. If your supervisor believes an EAP referral is necessary, he or she will call the EAP administrator in your presence. You are responsible for scheduling an appointment. The EAP will inform your supervisor whether or not you attended the session. The content of the appointment will remain confidential, unless you provide written consent to the contrary. Failure to attend a supervisor-referred EAP session may result in disciplinary action up to and including termination.

You may attend a supervisor-referred EAP appointment during business hours, with pay, by using your accrued sick time hours. Subsequent meetings and self-referrals should be scheduled for off- work hours, or you may use earned benefit time as approved by your supervisor.

Access to the EAP after Termination
Upon termination, employees and their families may use the EAP services for up to 60 days.

[AGENCY] has invested in an Employee Assistance Program and encourages its use as part of our commitment to help our employees in a professional and confidential manner. While employees are always encouraged to take advantage of the EAP, using EAP services does not mitigate the application of disciplinary measures under any circumstances. They are parallel courses of action.

For example, an employee might be having problems with absenteeism and tardiness. In this case, an appropriate role for the supervisor would be to discipline the employee, create a performance plan aimed at improvement and monitor the employee's progress. The supervisor might also remind the employee about the EAP by stating that personal issues can sometimes cause absenteeism and tardiness and that the EAP can help with these issues if they exist. The supervisor also should state that the employee's performance must improve, whether the individual chooses EAP services or not.

EAPs and Terminated Employees: Sometimes employees who abuse drugs and alcohol will be terminated. They will have engaged in gross misconduct or, after repeated interventions, continue to have performance or behavior problems in the workplace. Employers can still support these employees by encouraging them to use the services of the EAP even after termination.

See Also: Corporate Commitment to Employee Wellness; Access to Healthcare and Other Related Benefits; Drug Testing; Paid Time Off; Sick Time; Discipline; Return-to-Work Reintegration

Disclaimer: This policy should not substitute for independent legal review of local, State and Federal laws applicable to your agency. Consult an attorney prior to the implementation of any new organizational policy.

Short-Term Disability Policy

Disability insurance benefits, particularly short-term disability (STD) benefits, can be a helpful tool for organizations when intervening with staff with substance misuse issues. Short-term disability benefits provide some level of salary replacement when they are temporarily unable to perform core job functions because of a medical issue.

Providing STD benefits can be a cost-effective way to help employees seeking treatment. STD benefits relieve the agency of providing sick time benefits for these employees, which can be far more costly than the STD insurance premiums. Short-term disability benefits also give the employer an opportunity to develop a return-to-work strategy.

It is important to note that not all STD policies provide benefits for employees seeking addictions treatment. Employers who want to have such benefits should check with their insurance provider.

Components of a Retention-Oriented Short-Term Disability Policy

Organizations can use the components described below to develop, add to or enhance their existing policies.

Intervention

The following components can be incorporated into an STD Policy so that the organization can intervene with an individual who has a substance use problem and provide benefits for treatment or recovery support.

- Require application for STD benefits if absence extends beyond an established period of time
- Mandate the use of sick time and other paid time off prior to accessing STD benefits

Re- Entry

The following policy components allow an individual to return to work while protecting the organization and employee.

- Use of sick time after returning from STD leave must be medically confirmed with a doctor's note.
- Employees can come back to work on a modified schedule (subject to approval and other applicable policies).
- Employees must submit to a drug test to return to work.

Policy in Practice

The agency can leverage its relationship with an STD benefits provider to ensure that employees seeking services while on short-term disability are making consistent progress. Often the disability benefits company will be actively involved in contacting the service provider to help devise strategies for getting the employee back to work as effectively and efficiently as possible. In addition, many disability policies have a "mandatory rehabilitation" clause that requires employees who make a disability claim to go through a rehabilitation program approved by the insurance company, thus increasing the likelihood that employees who make a disability claim based on substance misuse will enter treatment.

Waiting/Elimination Period

The waiting or elimination period is the period of time that an employee must be out and unable to work before he or she is eligible for disability benefits. The role of sick time is critical here. While increasing the waiting/elimination period usually decreases premiums, it also generally results in increased use of sick time, which is the benefit typically used during the waiting/elimination period. Ultimately, expended sick time may cost the employer more than increased premiums.

Absences Requiring Short-Term Disability

Employees who have accrued a significant number of sick time hours may prefer to use that time for extended illnesses rather than apply for STD benefits, particularly if they have sick time hours beyond the STD waiting/elimination period. As a financial consideration, employers can discourage this practice by mandating STD application for medical absences beyond the waiting period. By doing so, employers will realize two benefits: First, they will maximize the efficiency of their investment in STD benefits. Second, once the employee is on STD, he or she must comply with the mandates from the disability insurance company in order to receive benefits. This arrangement allows agency staff to be more removed from the process of managing the employee's absence, while ensuring that the employee is complying with a structured plan for his or her return to work.

SAMPLE POLICY

Regular employees who meet the eligibility requirements including, but not limited to, length of service requirements, are eligible for short-term disability (STD) benefits. In the event that you become disabled due to a non-work-related illness or injury, you may qualify to receive these benefits. Short-term disability benefits represent a percentage of your gross weekly salary. The human resources department can give you specifics about the current policy, including eligibility requirements, elimination periods, carriers and benefits.

Waiting/Elimination Period

There is a waiting period (also known as an elimination period) before short- term disability benefits begin.

You will be required to use other paid time off, including sick time and personal time, if available, in order to receive pay during this elimination period.

Absence Not Requiring STD

If your illness or injury prevents you from attending work for less than the current elimination period, it is not necessary for you to apply for STD benefits. In this case, you may be allowed to use earned sick, vacation and personal time in order to be paid for this absence. If you do not have earned time, this period may be taken as unpaid leave. [AGENCY] reserves the right to ask for additional information from your healthcare provider and/or for additional medical opinions. Failure to provide adequate medical information or to submit to additional opinions may result in payroll adjustment and/or disciplinary action up to and including discharge or other appropriate action.

Absence Requiring STD

If your eligible absence extends beyond the elimination period, and you are eligible for STD benefits, you will be required to apply for them. In this case, you will be required to [*Insert necessary requirements for initiation of STD benefits according to the terms of your STD agreement.*]. Failure to comply with these requirements may result in payroll adjustment and/or disciplinary action. [*AGENCY*] reserves the right to ask for additional information from your health care provider and/or for additional medical opinions. Failure to provide adequate medical information or to submit to additional opinions may result in payroll adjustment and/or disciplinary action up to and including discharge or other appropriate action.

Notification Requirement

It is your responsibility to notify the human resources department if you will be absent for longer than five working days due to illness, accident or injury, or if you wish to apply for STD and you know in advance that you will be absent for more than the current elimination period.

STD and FMLA

All time used during the elimination period and while on STD will count toward the 12-week leave per calendar year allowable under the Family and Medical Leave Act of 1993. If your STD leave totals 12 weeks or less, you will be reinstated to the same (or a similar) position that you held prior to the STD leave. If your leave extends beyond the 12-week maximum, we cannot guarantee that a position will be available when you are ready to return.

Furnishing the Carrier with Information

Periodically, the insurance carrier may require additional or updated physician's information regarding your status. You must furnish this information immediately or benefits may be discontinued. If STD benefits are discontinued for any reason, you will be expected to return to work immediately with a doctor's release. Otherwise, the agency will assume that you have resigned your position retroactive to the last day for which STD benefits were received.

Supervisory and Human Resources Check-In

In addition to insurance carrier updates, you are also required to check in with human resources on a weekly basis. Your supervisor also may request that you periodically check in to keep him or her apprised of your work status and expected date of return. If your supervisor requests that you contact him or her on a routine basis during your absence, it is your responsibility to do so. Contacting only the human resources department does not fulfill your obligation to contact your supervisor if he or she requests that you do so. Failure to fulfill these responsibilities may result in disciplinary action up to and including discharge.

[AGENCY] reserves the right to ask for additional information from your healthcare provider and/or for additional medical opinions. Failure to provide adequate medical information or to submit to additional opinions may result in payroll adjustment and/or disciplinary action up to and including discharge or other appropriate action.

STD and Continuation of Health Benefits and Benefit Time

While you are out on approved short-term disability leave, your health benefits are continued for up to 12 consecutive weeks. If your leave extends beyond 12 weeks, you may continue your health insurance coverage through COBRA, which requires you to pay the full monthly premium charged by the insurance carrier.

Benefit time will continue to accrue as long as you return to active duty following your leave, but it will not be available for use until you return to work. If you do not return, benefit time accrued while you were on leave will be withdrawn retroactive to the date you were last at work

[NOTE: Your Short-Term Disability Policy may include other provisions, such as special circumstances or illnesses, relationship to long-term disability, and other considerations dictated by the specifics of your insurance policy.]

See Also: Access to Healthcare and Other Related Benefits; Paid Time Off; Sick Time; Family Medical Leave Act; Return-to-Work Reintegration

Disclaimer: This policy should not substitute for independent legal review of local, State and Federal laws applicable to your agency. Consult an attorney prior to the implementation of any new organizational policy.

Family and Medical Leave Act (FMLA) Policy

Note: For a general overview of the Family and Medical Leave Act and its overall relationship to substance misuse, please see "Summary of Relevant Federal Laws."

On January 8, 2008, President George W. Bush signed into law HR 4986, the National Defense Authorization Act (NDAA) for fiscal year 2008. Section 585 of this Act amends the FMLA to allow family members to take up to 26 work weeks of leave to care for " a member of the Armed Forces ... who is undergoing medical treatment, recuperation or therapy, is otherwise in outpatient status, or is otherwise on the temporary disability retired list for a serious injury or illness." The NDAA also permits an employee to take FMLA leave for any "qualifying exigency as the Secretary of Labor shall, by regulation, determine) arising out of the fact that a spouse son daughter or parent of the employee is on active duty (or has been notified of an impending call or order to active duty) . . ." The Secretary of Labor has not issued final regulations regarding this legislation. In the interim, employers are required to act in good faith in providing the appropriate leave.

A detailed guide to FMLA as well as an update on guidance regarding the new legislation can be found at http://www.dol.gov/esa/whd/fmla/index.htm.

The Family and Medical leave Act of 1993 requires that employers with more than 50 employees allow eligible employees to take an unpaid leave of up to 12 weeks a year under certain circumstances, such as the employee's own serious health condition. The law bars employers from taking any retaliatory action against an employee because he or she takes leave under the Act.

Employers with fewer than 50 employees are not legally required to comply with the Act. Small employers, however, may choose to offer leave for employees experiencing substance misuse issues by simply extending any existing leave policy to employees who seek services for a substance use problem.

FMLA allows eligible employees to take leave under the Act to go to treatment for drug or alcohol addiction. Thus, it is an important tool for intervening with employees experiencing difficulty related to substance misuse. In addition to providing leave, the Act stipulates that employees who return to work within the 12-week time frame be restored to their job or an equal position.

Although employees who are currently abusing substances are not protected under the Americans with Disabilities Act (see "Summary of Relevant Federal Laws regarding Substance Misuse in the Workplace"), it is advisable to keep policies covering leave for substance abuse issues as consistent as possible with other medical leave policies, thereby eliminating any potential claim of discrimination. As always, agencies should consult an attorney before publishing or implementing new personnel policies.

Components of a Retention-Oriented FMLA Policy

An employer's FMLA Policy is largely governed by the requirements of the law itself. This section is intended to emphasize key FMLA components. Smaller organizations can use the concepts behind FMLA and learn from the way in which the law is applied.

Employee Eligibility

Employee eligibility for leave under FMLA and the amount of leave available vary based on employee tenure. The US Department of Labor Web site is helpful for determining eligibility requirements (www.dol.gov/esa/whd/fmla/index.htm/). Employers are free to extend leave benefits beyond the law, even to employees who may not technically qualify under FMLA.

Time-Limited Leave/Frequency of Leave

FMLA allows for up to 12–weeks of leave per year. The employer can define when that year begins and ends (calendar, fiscal, etc.). Any definition that is used should be consistent regardless of the reason for the leave. The Act allows 12 weeks to be taken consecutively or on an intermittent basis.

Employee Responsibilities While on Leave

The employee should be required to maintain reasonable contact with the company (either his or her direct supervisor or the human resources department – depending on the size of the company. The frequency of this contact can vary based on circumstances such as where the employee is during leave (for example, in an inpatient treatment unit vs. at home and going to outpatient treatment) and how long the employee has been out on leave. Contact may be less frequent at the beginning of the leave and more frequent at the end or vice versa, depending on the circumstances. In general, contact should be by telephone until the employee is ready to return to work.

Provide Continued Medical Certification

As with any other medical leave, employees should be required to provide continued verification that the leave is medically necessary. Companies who offer short-term disability benefits for employees who are in treatment might want their STD insurance carrier to require and receive all medical certifications until the employee is ready to return to work. If the company does not have STD insurance, then the human resources department or a supervisor should require and receive medical certification as deemed necessary and appropriate. For smaller companies, it is recommended that a manager other than the employee's direct supervisor require and receive the certifications. Failure to provide the certifications as required should lead to the leave being disallowed, which helps assure the employer that the employee continues to be engaged in a recovery process and is working toward being able to return to work.

Return to Work

Under FMLA, employees who are medically able to return to work and who return after 12 weeks or less of leave must return to their original job or an equal position. For more information, about return-to-work requirements and procedures, see [AGENCY'S] Return to Work Policy. To avoid violations of the Americans with Disabilities Act, it is recommended that organizations employ standard return-to- work requirements for all employees who take leave for a medical concern.

SAMPLE FMLA/LEAVE POLICY

[NOTE: The policy below incorporates concepts related to use or misuse by an employee. The Act also covers family members. Conditions and policies applicable to leave taken to care for a family member should be included in your policy manual after consultation with legal counsel]

In accordance with the provisions of the Family and Medical Leave Act of 1993, you may be eligible for up to a total of 12 weeks of leave per calendar year under the following circumstances:

- For the birth, adoption or foster care placement of a child
- When needed to care for a spouse, child or parent with a serious health condition
- When unable to perform your job because of a serious health condition

Definition of Serious Health Condition

For the purposes of FMLA, a serious health condition is defined as an illness, injury, impairment, or physical or mental condition that involves: 1) a period of incapacity or treatment in connection with inpatient care, 2) a period of incapacity requiring absence from work, school or other regular activities for more than three days and that also involves continuing treatment by a healthcare provider, or 3) continuing treatment for prenatal care or for a chronic or long-term condition that is incurable and so serious that, if not treated, would likely result in a period of incapacity of three or more days.

Eligibility

To be eligible for FMLA leave you must have been employed at [AGENCY] for at least 12 months AND must have worked at least 1,250 hours during the 12-month period preceding the start of the leave. An exception will be made if the leave is for a medically certified personal serious health condition that would otherwise be eligible for FMLA leave. In these instances, all requirements regarding requesting leave, certification, return-to-work issues, etc., as outlined in this policy apply.

Leave Entitlement

If eligible, you are entitled to a maximum of 12 weeks of FMLA leave per calendar year. The 12 weeks need not be taken consecutively. When medically necessary, you may take intermittent leave for the serious health condition of your spouse, child, parent or self. Leave for voluntary treatments and procedures are not covered by the Act. All requests for continuous or intermittent FMLA leave for a serious health condition, whether the condition is yours or a family member's (as outlined in the Act), must be verified in writing as medically necessary by the attending physician (see "Medical Certification" below).

Once you have exhausted the 12-week maximum, no further FMLA leave will be allowed during that calendar year. To the extent it is still available; however, short-term disability benefits may apply.

Paid and Unpaid Leave

Leave requested for your own serious health condition must be charged against earned sick time, paid time off and short-term disability benefits (if an elimination period is required), before unpaid leave will be granted. The human resources department can give you details regarding how benefit time, if applicable, is paid. Both paid leave (using of sick time, paid time off or short-term disability benefits) and unpaid leave count toward the 12-week maximum leave allowed per calendar year. All time off for short-term disability or workers' compensation leave will be counted towards FMLA leave automatically.

Job and Benefits Protection

Upon your return from leave, you will be reinstated to the same (or a similar) position that you held prior to the leave. If your leave extends beyond the 12-week maximum, we cannot guarantee that a position will be available when you are ready to return.

While you are on approved FMLA leave, your health benefits may be continued for up to 12 consecutive weeks. If your leave extends beyond 12 weeks, you may elect COBRA continuation coverage and pay the full monthly premium cost charged by the insurance carrier.

While you are on approved leave, benefit time will continue to accrue as long as you return to active duty following your leave, but the time will not be available for use until your return. If you do not return, benefit time accrued while you were on leave will be withdrawn retroactive to the date you were last at work.

Requesting Family and Medical Leave

If the need for FMLA leave is foreseeable, you must provide your supervisor and the human resources department with at least 30 days written notice. If the circumstances are not foreseeable, notice must be provided as soon as possible. Written notice must include the reason for, dates and length of the requested leave, and must be accompanied by medical certification (as appropriate) as described below.

Medical Certification

[AGENCY] requires medical certification to support all requests for FMLA leave (continuous or intermittent) of more than one week. If there is a question about the adequacy of the medical certification, [AGENCY] may require additional medical opinions, at [AGENCY]'s expense, or more information from your healthcare provider. Failure to present adequate medical certification by the required date may result in denial of the request, a payroll adjustment, and/or disciplinary action up to and including discharge or other appropriate action. Refusal to consent to a request for additional medical opinions may result in denial of the leave request.

Return to Work

If you have taken FMLA leave for your own serious health condition, you will be required to provide adequate fitness-for-duty certification prior to your return to work. Your return to work must be accompanied by doctor's release. You may not work until a release is received. Your supervisor may send you home without pay until you can produce a release. If your supervisor sends you home, you must return with a release within 24 hours or the agency will assume that you have resigned your position.

[*AGENCY*] may ask for additional documentation from your healthcare provider and/or for additional medical opinions, which [*AGENCY*] may have sought at its own cost. Failure to provide adequate clearance as requested by the agency or to submit to additional opinions may result in payroll adjustment and/or disciplinary action up to and including discharge or other appropriate action.

See Also: Summary of Relevant Federal Laws; Access to Healthcare and Other Related Benefits; Paid Time Off; Sick Time; Short-Term Disability; Return-to-Work Reintegration

Disclaimer: This policy should not substitute for independent legal review of local, State and Federal laws applicable to your agency. Consult an attorney prior to the implementation of any new organizational policy.

Discipline Policy

A Discipline Policy is an articulation of interventions related to unsatisfactory employee performance and behavior. Generally, a Discipline Policy will be "progressive," meaning it reflects increasingly serious repercussions for continued poor performance or for more egregious violations.

A Discipline Policy covers a range of unacceptable behavior, including substance misuse in the workplace. The policy provides a means to intervene with employees who are misusing substances and experiencing performance or behavior problems on the job.

Components of a Retention-Oriented Discipline Policy

Organizations can use the components described below to develop, add to or enhance their existing policies.

Intervention

Including the following components in a Discipline Policy enables an organization to intervene when a substance use problem arises.

- Progressive levels of discipline
- Managerial discretion to invoke a level of discipline commensurate with the violation
- Managerial discretion to invoke training, education and referral options (for example, an EAP referral) as an adjunct to the disciplinary process

Policy in Practice

A common misconception among both employees and managers is that discipline is used solely to punish wrongdoing. According to the *American Heritage Dictionary*, however, the primary definition of discipline is "training that is expected to produce a specified character or pattern of behavior." Effective disciplinary processes are aimed at changing behavior or improving performance and should include training and education in addition to sanctions.

Two problems may arise out of the misconception of discipline as punishment. The first is avoidance of disciplinary actions to avoid a hostile confrontation, and the second is that disciplinary action often becomes overly focused on the process – for example, collecting documentation – and not on the underlying causes of the behavior. In addition, the supervisor may ignore smaller behavior or performance issues – even if they are reflective of a larger problem – to avoid the appearance of trying to "get employees in trouble." Not surprisingly, however, avoiding the small issues tends to enable underlying problems, which may go unchecked until they become problematic enough to dictate termination.

At the heart of this issue, is the need to re-double efforts to train supervisors and managers adequately so that they have a full range of skills to provide adequate time and structure for management and supervision.

Progressive discipline – discipline that moves from small interventions to larger ones – is a critical part of a workplace structure that encourages supervisors to intervene early rather than wait until a problem escalates. A progressive disciplinary process should provide education and training opportunities to all employees on how to improve performance and behavior. For example, an employee who violates the confidentiality code could be given a written warning about the violation and an assignment to attend additional confidentiality training or to review the confidentiality training materials and discuss them with the supervisor at a follow up meeting.

SAMPLE POLICY

[*AGENCY*] employees must meet reasonable expectations for performance and conduct. These expectations are determined by [*AGENCY*] and your supervisor and established through policies, procedures and rules. When an employee fails to meet these expectations or violates an agency rule or policy, disciplinary action up to and including discharge may be warranted.

Disciplinary action, while presented here in a progressive manner, is at the discretion of the supervisor, who may determine which action is applicable, fair and consistent based upon the frequency and/or severity of the infraction(s). Options available to your supervisor and standard ways you may respond include:

Oral Warning: An oral warning may be the first formal warning an employee receives for an infraction of a minor nature. Oral warnings also are put in writing and are signed by the employee. The employee may include his/her comments. Written documentation of an oral warning does not imply a written warning. The employee signature does not indicate that he or she agrees with the warning, only that he or she acknowledges receipt of the warning.

Written Warning: A written warning may be issued for an infraction of a more serious nature, as a second warning following an oral warning, or when one or more unrelated incidents have been addressed previously. Written warnings are signed by the employee. The employee may include his or her comments in the documentation. The employee signature does not indicate that he or she agrees with the warning, only that he or she acknowledges receipt of the warning.

Probation: Probation may be indicated for repeated violations of a minor nature, for violations of a more serious nature, or when there is a history of incidents (related or unrelated) that have been addressed previously. Probation also may be indicated when a written warning has already been issued. Failure to successfully complete the probation period may result in discharge. Written documentation including the employee's signature should be in place at the start of the probation period. The employee is not guaranteed continued employment for the full probation period.

Suspension: Suspension may be indicated for repeated violations of a minor nature, for violations of a more serious nature, or when there is a history of incidents (related or unrelated) have been addressed previously. Suspension also may be indicated when a written warning has already been issued. Upon return from suspension, the employee will be placed on probation automatically. Written documentation including the employee's signature should be in place at the start of a suspension.

Discharge: Discharge is the ultimate disciplinary action for violations of a serious nature or repeated actions of a minor nature. Certain acts of misconduct or violations of rules or policy may justify immediate discharge.

When dealing with a substance misuse issue, an EAP referral can be an appropriate adjunct to the disciplinary process. Like the Discipline Policy itself, an EAP referral can be applied progressively, beginning with the manager reminding the employee that the EAP exists all the way to the manager making a mandatory referral.

It is important to note that while a Discipline Policy lays out the philosophy and practice of progressive discipline, it leaves the door open for immediate termination in appropriate cases. There is no set number of warnings or disciplinary actions before a termination (for example, "three strikes"). A Discipline Policy must allow for managerial discretion depending on the number, nature and severity of infractions.

Employers also need to keep the idea of precedent in mind when implementing disciplinary procedures. If one employee is terminated for a specific behavior while another receives an oral warning for the same behavior, the employer may be vulnerable to legal action unless there is a significant difference in the circumstances surrounding the two employees or incidents.

See Also: Code of Professional Conduct; Employee Assistance Program

Disclaimer: This policy should not substitute for independent legal review of local, State and Federal laws applicable to your agency. Consult an attorney prior to the implementation of any new organizational policy.

IV. OTHER TOOLS

Return-to-Work Reintegration Plan

Management Practice Guidelines

A return-to-work plan provides an outline of conditions under which an employee may be allowed to return to work following a leave related to substance misuse. Issues surrounding return to work after use or misuse can present an agency with significant challenges. A sound, clear return-to-work strategy is critical to reintegrating employees into their full responsibilities of their job. A return-to-work plan includes:

- A certification of **fitness for duty** indicating that the employee is able to return to work
- A **return-to-duty** contract that the employee signs and follows
- **Supervisory guidelines** for monitoring the employee when he or she returns to work

Key Legal Issues

Three important Federal laws relate to employees who return to work after a leave of absence during which they sought substance use treatment: the Americans with Disabilities Act (ADA) of 1990, the Americans with Disabilities Amendments Act of 2008 (effective January 2009) and the Family and Medical Leave Act (FMLA).

Employees who seek treatment for addiction are protected against workplace discrimination under the American with Disabilities Act. Employees who return to work after having such an episode *must be treated similarly to employees who return to work after taking medical leave for any other physical or mental health condition.* ADA protection does not apply to employees who are *currently* misusing drugs.

Employees who take a medical leave under FMLA are granted job security under the Act. FMLA stipulates that if the employee is medically able to return to work within 12 weeks and does so, he or she must be restored to his or her former position or an equal position. As defined under the law, "equal position" means similar title, pay, status, responsibilities, conditions, qualifications, authority and no significant increase in commuting time or distance.

Fundamental Components of a Return-to-Work Plan

Fitness-for-Duty Certification

All returning employees (from FMLA or other leave) must present a fitness-for- duty certification stating that he or she is able to return to work and perform essential job functions. In the case of employees returning after a leave due to substance misuse, it is recommended that the employer require the following evidence of fitness to return to duty:

Evidence that the employee completed a course of primary treatment, counseling or other recovery support service as appropriate.

The employee should be required to present some evidence that he or she completed a course of appropriate treatment or recovery support while on leave. Employers do not need to determine, nor should they determine, what services are appropriate. The employee simply should be required to show that he or she was involved in and *successfully completed* some form of treatment or recovery support service.

Evidence that the employee's treatment or service provider certifies that he or she is able to perform the essential functions of the job

The foremost question most employers have when an employee comes back from medical leave is, "He/She was not able to do her a job for a time because of her health condition. Can he/she do her job now?" This question can be answered best by the employee's healthcare provider. One of the best ways to secure an answer is to have the provider review the employee's job description and certify whether he or she is able to perform the essential functions of the job – as indicated on the job description – with or without restriction or accommodation. The provider should supply written certification of the individual's capacity to complete job functions and any special conditions. If the employee can perform his/her essential functions with some sort of accommodation, the provider should describe the accommodation. Employers can require that the healthcare providers who supply the fitness-for-duty certifications meet certain requirements (for example, hold a license or certification to provide substance abuse counseling).

Temporary re-assignment to a non-clinical position is one of the accommodations the returning employee might request. Under the Americans with Disabilities Act, the employer is required to consider such a request, but the law does not require the employer to grant the request if it would place an undue burden on the employer. Some agencies (mostly larger ones with more flexibility) may be able to temporarily grant accommodation requests; other agencies, however, may not have that ability.

If the employee's provider asks for an accommodation to enable the employee to perform the essential functions of his or her job, the employer may (but does not have to) require the provider to produce a diagnosis indicating that the employee is in remission. Diagnostic information should not be requested, however, unless the employee seeks an accommodation.

Under the Americans with Disabilities Act, the employer must engage in a conversation with the employee regarding whether or not accommodations might be made. The employer must consider any accommodation requested and determine if it can be granted or if it poses an undue burden on the employer. As always, it is advisable to consult with legal counsel before denying a request for a reasonable accommodation. Employers should always keep in mind the concept of precedent. If an accommodation has been made in the past, it is reasonable for an employee to believe that it can be made in the future.

In addition, the employer can have its own healthcare representative (for example, the organization's medical director or EAP provider) contact the employee's healthcare provider for clarification. The employer's healthcare representative can ask for authentication of the provider's qualifications. If the employer's healthcare representative questions the authenticity of the employee's healthcare provider, the employer can request that the employee be certified by a healthcare professional of the employer's choosing (and potentially at the employer's cost). Whoever performs these functions should meet or exceed the qualifications required of the employee's healthcare provider. Under no circumstances should the return-to-work certification be performed by the employee's direct supervisor.

Return-to-Work Conditions

After the employee has provided fitness-for-duty certification, it is recommended that the employee be required to:

- **Pass a drug test.** Even if the treatment provider or other professional who completed the fitness-for-duty statement performed a drug test, it is recommended that an additional drug test be given immediately before the employee comes back to work. The agency's EAP provider usually can perform or facilitate such tests.
- **Sign a return-to-duty contract** (sample included). Because of the nature of work performed in the addictions field, employers have a legitimate right, indeed a responsibility, to ensure that clinical employees and employees who have managerial responsibilities related to clinical services are drug free. While employers would not require that all employees returning from medical leave submit to random drug testing, it is acceptable and recommended that employees who return to service delivery after a leave related to substance misuse be required to submit to random drug testing for a period of up to 60 months. This length of time is consistent among industries and positions considered to be safety sensitive.

  The return-to-duty contract also can include a provision stating that the employee must continue his or her involvement with continuing care, self–help, or treatment and/or recovery support services as recommended by the service provider. The EAP (or someone other than the employee's direct supervisor) can monitor these services. The contract can read that failure to participate in recommended services may result in disciplinary action up to and including termination. If such a provision is added to the contract, the only information that the supervisor should receive is the fact of the employee's participation in recommended services, not the nature or quality of the participation.
- **Provide documentation that the basic qualifications for the position the employee is returning to are met** (for example, his or her license or certification is still current; drivers' license is still valid, etc.).

Return-to-Work Supervision Commensurate with Pre-Leave Performance and Behavior

It is not uncommon for an employee to experience job performance problems, such as absenteeism, erratic behavior, and decreased performance or productivity, before he or she goes on leave for substance misuse. Medical leave may occur during the intervention process. When the employee returns to work, disciplinary action and performance plans should pick up where they left off. In other words, taking a leave does not negate prior behavior nor does it clean the slate of disciplinary actions or performance plans enacted prior to the leave.

SAMPLE: RETURN-TO-DUTY CONTRACT

I, _____, hereby understand and accept the following conditions of employment at [AGENCY]. I further understand that failure to comply with any of these conditions will be considered grounds for immediate termination.

- I must remain drug and alcohol free.
- I will schedule and attend all supervisor-referred Employee Assistance Program appointments.
- I will attend all treatment, self-help or other recovery support services recommended by the Employee Assistance Program.
- I will be required to pass a drug test prior to my returning to work (if I have been on leave).
- I will be required to submit to random drug tests for up to 60 months. A positive drug test or failure to immediately provide a sample for testing will be considered grounds for immediate termination of employment.

The conditions of this contract will be reviewed after a period of six months.

_____   _____
Employee   Date

_____   _____
Manager   Date

The medical certification stating that an employee needs a temporary leave indicates that he or she is temporarily unable to perform the functions of the job. The fitness-for-duty statement indicates that he or she is once again able to perform essential functions of the job. As a result, upon return from leave, the employee is expected to perform his or her job adequately, barring specific accommodations as described above.

In addition to implementing the return-to-duty contract to help ensure that returning employees remain drug free, the agency should supervise returning employees at a level commensurate with their behavior and performance prior to their taking leave. Because employees returning to work from additions treatment are protected by the Americans with Disabilities Act, they should return under conditions similar to those required of employees who have been away due to other disabilities. At the same time, employers want to make sure that employees can and are performing their jobs adequately. The key to avoiding ADA problems in the return-to-work process is to make sure that supervision levels and methods are dictated by employee behavior and performance, not by the nature of the employee's disability.

See Also: Access to Healthcare and Other Related Benefits; Drug Testing; Employee Assistance Program; Family Medical Leave Act (FMLA)

Disclaimer: This policy should not substitute for independent legal review of local, State and Federal laws applicable to your agency. Consult an attorney prior to the implementation of any new organizational policy.

Using Client Feedback as a Management Tool

Outreach to Clients

Client feedback is a way to ensure the quality of service delivery. Client feedback can help identify staff behaviors that may indicate the presence of substance use or misuse or other stressors. While the general purpose of client feedback is to assess performance of direct service staff, other staff with whom the client interacts also may be included.

Tool in Practice

Clients may be the first to realize that staff members are struggling with personal issues. It is not uncommon for addictions professionals to have as much, if not more, contact with clients as they have with fellow professionals during the work day. It is a good practice to have a formal process in place by which clients can provide feedback regarding their interaction with staff. This process should be separate from a formal client rights and responsibilities process, which clearly states the steps that clients should go through if they have complaints.

Client outreach involves regularly contacting clients, either by phone or in person, to give them an opportunity to comment generally about their experience with the agency. This process should involve a standard set of open- ended questions about the client's interactions with staff. If client outreach is used, it must be done in a standardized way across the agency. Clients should be contacted on a random basis to avoid particular employees from being singled out.

SAMPLE TOOL: CLIENT OUTREACH QUESTIONNAIRE

Hi, my name is _____. I'm a (supervisor at/I work in the quality assurance department at/I am the director of) _____ agency. From time to time, we contact clients to find out more about their experiences at our agency.

Would you be willing to talk to me for a few minutes about how things are going for you in your treatment?

How is the staff treating you?

Is the person who answers our phone polite when you call?

Does your counselor return your phone calls?

Do our staff members treat you the way you want to be treated?

If not, can you tell me more about that?

Would you recommend that a family or friend seek treatment at our agency?

I'd like to give you my number. If you ever want to talk to me, please give me a call.

V. CASE STUDIES: TOOLS IN ACTION

Case Study: Using Multiple Tools

Sonya has had performance problems in the last 60 days, including unauthorized absences and tardiness. Yesterday, her supervisor overheard Sonya yelling at a client on the phone after he missed a group session. She was loud and clinically inappropriate, but she did not swear or threaten the client.

Sonya has worked at the agency for two years and has performed at or slightly above expectation for most of that time.

The Response: A written warning (or separate warnings) for the tardiness, absenteeism and yelling at the client along with a performance plan might be an appropriate supervisory intervention at this point. In addition, the supervisor might remind Sonya about the EAP and encourage her to attend. The supervisor could simply state that this kind of behavior at work can be due to something else going on in the employee's life and the EAP exists to help. Note that at this point, the EAP is *suggested* as a resource for the employee.

Two weeks later, the supervisor receives a call from a local probation officer who complains that he called Sonya about a report he needed on one of her clients who is on his caseload. He says he needed to report to a judge on the client's progress and didn't have the necessary information. He explains that the report is due at the same time every month (a week ago), and that Sonya had not sent it to him. The probation officer complains that Sonya "went off on him on the phone" and that she told him he would get his report when she was "ready to give it to him." Upon investigation, the supervisor discovers that Sonya has not written the report. Co-workers whose desks are next to Sonya's overheard the altercation with the probation officer on the phone and describe it as loud and unprofessional.

At this point in the progressive discipline process, Sonya's supervisor may want to think about a short disciplinary suspension and make a supervisory referral to the EAP related to Sonya's behavior.

Two days later, Sonya is back after a one-day suspension. Two days after her return from suspension, she takes a 90-minute lunch break. When she comes back to the office, she falls asleep at her desk. At this point, the supervisor suspects that substance misuse may be an issue. In the last several weeks, Sonya has:

- Been absent and tardy several times
- Had a verbal altercation with a client and a probation officer
- Failed to write a mandatory report to the court
- Taken a long lunch and fallen asleep at her desk afterwards

Taken together, these behaviors cause the supervisor to be concerned about substance misuse. Based on the agency's Drug Testing Policy, the supervisor feels she has reasonable cause to require a drug test from Sonya.

The Response: The supervisor calls Sonya into the office and briefly outlines her concerns about Sonya's behavior over the past few months. (Tip: Since a meeting like this may be volatile or end in termination, it is a good idea to have someone else present – a human resources representative, another supervisor or the supervisor's supervisor).

Sonya's supervisor outlines the recent behavior and performance issues that concern her and explains that she is concerned that drug or alcohol misuse might be an issue. Sonya denies this. The supervisor asks her to submit to a drug test. Sonya refuses. The supervisor points out that even if the test is positive, Sonya would not be fired; rather, she would be encouraged to seek treatment, the agency would hold her job for up to 12 weeks and, if she's ready to return in that time, the agency would do its best to help her come back. Sonya then admits that she has been using drugs for the past eight weeks. Because Sonya self-reported her drug use, a drug test is no longer necessary.

At this point, the supervisor should outline the company's general policy:

- Sonya cannot work while she is using drugs (See Drug Testing and Drug-Free Workplace policies).
- Sonya can take leave for up to 12 weeks.

The agency should encourage Sonya to go to treatment and/or get involved in other recovery support-activities. If Sonya wants to take leave with the hope of returning, the supervisor should immediately make a mandatory referral to the EAP in Sonya's presence. When Sonya is ready to return to work, she must: (See FMLA Policy and Return to Work Guidelines)

- Provide documentation that she completed treatment or other recovery support services
- Show medical certification that she is medically able to return to work
- Provide a negative drug test (See also Drug Testing policy)
- Sign a contract requiring abstinence and an individualized return-to-work plan (See also Drug Testing policy)

Case Studies: Drug-Free Workplace

Employee A is an accountant in the agency's finance department. At dinner with her husband on a weekday evening, she has two glasses of wine.

She comes to work the next day on time and performs her duties adequately. She tells her co-workers at lunch that she and her husband tried a new restaurant the night before and, because the restaurant had such an extensive wine list, she tried two different types of wine with her dinner.

The Response: The employee has not violated policy. Her work was not impaired and neither the mission nor reputation of the agency was threatened.

Employee B is an agency counselor. She has disclosed over time that she is in recovery. One day, she leaves work and goes to a restaurant/bar a half block from the agency. The restaurant employees know where she works because agency staff often goes to the restaurant for lunch. The employee stays at the bar for several hours and leaves clearly intoxicated. A waitress at the bar (who is a member of a 12-step program) comes to the agency the next day and reports this situation to the director. The employee is two hours late for work the next day, calling in to say her car won't start.

The Response: In this instance, the agency could regard the employee's off-duty behavior as both impairing her ability to perform her job (she was two hours late to work) and threatening the reputation of the agency. She is a treatment counselor openly in recovery who went to a bar a half a block from the program and became intoxicated.

Employee C is the quality assurance (QA) specialist for a large treatment program. As a reward for outstanding work over the last year, the agency sends her to a conference in Florida. The conference includes staff from substance abuse, child welfare, public health and other social service agencies from around the country. On the first night of the conference, the employee joins a large group of attendees in the hotel bar. She and others stay in the bar drinking heavily until closing at 1 a.m. The group then goes to one of the attendee's rooms and continues to drink until 2:30 a.m., when hotel security is called with a noise complaint.

Two days later, another employee who was at the conference tells the agency director about the incident. The other employee was with the QA specialist until she left the bar. He saw security break up the party in the hotel room later because his room was on the same floor. He describes the employee's behavior at the time as loud and intoxicated. The other employee says that the QA specialist attended the plenary session the next morning and was seen in conference workshops the next day.

The Response: In this example, the QA specialist violated the Drug-Free Workplace Policy because she was at a professional conference representing the agency. Her alcohol use, while it did not impair her ability to perform her job the next day, threatened the agency's reputation.

Case Studies: Return to Work/Reasonable Accommodations

Employee A went on leave under FMLA and completed 28-days of inpatient treatment followed by 60 days of intensive outpatient treatment. She has used her 12 weeks of FMLA leave. She has taken and passed a drug test. She has certification that she completed the inpatient and intensive outpatient treatment programs. She has a fitness-for-duty statement indicating that she can perform the essential functions of her job. She is requesting an accommodation to allow her to use flex-time benefits for a period of 60 days so she can attend her outpatient group session at 3 p.m. twice a week.

The Response: In practice, this request means the employee would leave the office at 2:30 p.m. and return at 4:30 p.m. twice a week. She can make up the two hours she misses by staying at work until 7 p.m. on those days. This accommodation is likely one that the employer would be able to grant.

Employee B went to treatment and has been out for 12 weeks. He says that he is ready to return to work. He has passed a drug test and has provided documentation that he completed intensive outpatient treatment. His fitness-for-duty statement says he can perform the essential functions of his job, but he is asking to return to work part time (60%) on a permanent basis. The agency's EAP representative contacts the employee's treatment provider who says that he reviewed the employee's job description and believes that working full time is too stressful him at this time and would threaten his sobriety.

The Response: Unless a part-time position is available or feasible, this accommodation might be considered an undue burden on the employer.

Employee C works as an intake worker in a methamphetamine unit in a prison-based treatment program. She has been on medical leave for three months. She went to 30 days of intensive outpatient treatment followed by 60 days of outpatient treatment after she began abusing methamphetamine. She has provided her return-to-work fitness–or-duty statement, which indicates that she completed the 30-day program. She has provided a clean drug test.

The employee's treatment provider reviews her job description and requests that she not work with methamphetamine clients. The employee does not want to work in a prison setting because she feels doing so will put her sobriety at risk. The agency runs a community-based program that is not specifically designed for methamphetamine clients, however, there are no available intake- worker positions, and the employee does not have the qualifications necessary to be a counselor.

The Response: This accommodation is not likely to be granted because it creates an undue burden on the agency.

Employee D goes to treatment after his supervisor refers him to the EAP for erratic behavior in the workplace. In his second session with the EAP provider, the employee admits to having relapsed. After being on leave for 10 weeks and attending various treatment and recovery support services, he asks to return to his former position as a senior counselor. He provides a clean drug test and verification that he has been involved with recovery support services. His treatment or recovery support service provider has reviewed his job description and indicates that he can perform the essential functions of his job.

While the employee was on leave, however, his certification as a certified substance abuse counselor expired. The State certification board indicates that he is 100 training hours short. It is a State licensure requirement that senior counselors be certified.

The Response: The employee cannot return to his position without his certification, and the agency is not required to provide him a position that does not necessitate certification. If such a position exists and is open and available, the agency may choose to allow him to transfer into that position.

Case Studies: Return to Work/Supervision Levels

Case 1: Sonya, whose case is outlined above, had a number of performance issues before she admitted to drug use. She was referred to the EAP and took leave under FLMA to attend treatment. She completed 28-days of inpatient treatment and then, while still on leave from work, attended intensive outpatient treatment for another month. After providing a fitness-for-duty certification and a clean drug test, she will return to work.

Before Sonya left, she received a written warning for tardiness, absenteeism and yelling at a client. She received a second warning and a one-day suspension for yelling at a probation officer. After the suspension, she took a long lunch and fell asleep at her desk. At that point, she admitted to using drugs and alcohol. Before she left, Sonya was facing possible termination for all of the above issues.

The Response: When Sonya comes back to work, these disciplinary actions will remain in her file; she will not return with a clean slate. Sonya should be monitored closely for a period of time commensurate with the length of time this behavior would be monitored for any other employee.

Case 2: Ted is returning to work after a leave during which he went to intensive outpatient treatment. Before he left, he had called in sick two days in a row because he was on a binge. The following Monday, he neither came to work nor called in. On Tuesday, Ted was standing at his supervisor's door when she arrived at work. He told her about the binge the previous week and explained that was why he had failed to come to work the day before. He said he had contacted his sponsor and was working on enrolling in a treatment program. He requested FMLA leave. Before leaving, he met with his supervisor to discuss his caseload. He has been on leave for 60 days and has provided his fitness-for-duty certification and a clean drug test.

The Response: Ted's return-to-work supervision should be commensurate with the behavior that led to his leaving. He had absenteeism problems but quickly came to his supervisor, discussed his situation, briefed her on his clients and got into treatment before his behavior was overly problematic.

APPENDIX A. SUMMARY OF RELEVANT FEDERAL LAWS

This section provides an overview of relevant Federal employment and workplace laws as they apply in the context of employee substance use and misuse and agency responses to this activity. This section does not represent a legal opinion, nor does it include any State laws that also may apply. Any formal employment policy implemented by an organization should be reviewed by legal counsel.

Drug-Free Workplace Act of 1988

The Drug-Free Workplace Act of 1988 requires any organization that receives a Federal contract of $100,000 or more or a Federal grant of any amount to have a drug-free workplace policy. Specifically, the Act requires that the organization develop and distribute a formal drug-free workplace policy prohibiting the manufacture, use or sale of substances. It also requires establishment of a prevention-oriented awareness program, including information about the dangers of substance use and about options for intervention. In addition, it requires specific activities related to the Federal contract, including notifications to the employer and to the contracting agency that an employee has been convicted of a drug-law violation. Finally, the Act requires that the employer respond to violations of the drug-free workplace policy, whether through disciplinary action, referrals to treatment or both.

Americans with Disabilities Act of 1990

The Americans with Disabilities Act of 1990 (ADA) prohibits employers with more than 15 employees from discriminating against applicants and employees because of a physical and/or mental disability. The ADA does not protect employees who are currently using illicit substances but does protect those in recovery who have sought treatment. This protection means that in all management and personnel matters, an agency cannot treat employees who are in substance use treatment or have participated in treatment differently from other employees simply on the basis of their involvement in treatment. Disciplinary policies and requirements for reinstatement must be applied equally to all returning employees.

Perhaps the most explicit application of the ADA in the context of use and misuse is drug testing. A supervisor must have reasonable cause to suspect an employee is using substances before requiring a drug test. A history that includes treatment and recovery cannot be a contributing factor to determining reasonable cause. For example, employees A and B are both late for work three times in two weeks.

Employee A is openly in recovery; employee B does not have a history of drug use. The supervisor cannot mandate a drug test for employee A because he believes that he or she is more likely to be using substances.

Americans with Disabilities Amendments Act of 2008

The recently enacted Americans with Disabilities Amendments Act (ADAA) became effective January1, 2009. The purpose of the amendments is to clarify that the provisions of the ADA should be broadly interpreted. Below is a summary of the provisions of the Amendments. Because of the Amendments recent enactment, they have not yet been tested.

It is important to note that the Amendments suggest a broad definition of disability. While the definition of "disability" remains "a physical or mental impairment that substantially limits one or more major life activities; a record of having such an impairment; or being regarded as having such an impairment," the Amendments broaden the definition of "major life activities" by stating that such activities include, but are not limited to, caring for oneself, performing manual tasks, seeing, hearing, eating, sleeping, walking, standing, lifting, bending, speaking, breathing, learning, reading, concentrating, thinking, communicating, and working. People in recovery often have problems with many of these activities – for example, sleeping, concentrating, thinking and working. However, having a problem may or may not mean that a person has an impairment that substantially limits a major life activity. To be disabled, the ADA requires that a person has an impairment that substantially limits a major life activity.

The Amendments also state that a major life activity includes the operation of major bodily functions, such as functions of the immune system, normal cell growth, digestive, bowel, bladder, neurological, brain, circulatory, endocrine, and reproductive systems. Addiction can cause physical problems in some of these areas, which can endure long past the time that substance misuse ends.

The Amendments also provide that:

- The definition of disability should be broadly construed.
- Mitigating measures other than ordinary eyeglasses or contact lenses shall not be considered in assessing whether an individual has a disability.
- An impairment that is episodic or in remission is a disability if it would substantially limit a major life activity when active.

A detailed guide to the ADA can be found at http://www.usdoj.gov/crt/ada/adahom1.htm/.

Family and Medical Leave Act of 1993

The Family and Medical Leave Act of 1993 (FMLA) applies to organizations with more than 50 employees. FMLA allows employees with at least one year of tenure to take up to 12 weeks of unpaid leave because of a serious health problem, including substance use, and allows them to return to the same or an equivalent position within the organization. FMLA applies to an employee's medical conditions as well as to care for a close family member undergoing treatment for a medical condition.

Additionally, on January 28, 2008, President George W. Bush signed into law HR 4986, the National Defense Authorization Act (NDAA) for fiscal year 2008. Section 585 of this Act amends the FMLA to allow family members to take up to 26 work weeks of leave to care for a member of the Armed Forces who is undergoing medical treatment, recuperation or therapy, is otherwise in outpatient status, or is otherwise on the temporary disability retired list for a serious injury or illness. The NDAA also permits an employee to take FMLA leave for any qualifying exigency as the Secretary of Labor shall, by regulation, determine arising out of the fact that a spouse, son, daughter, or parent of the employee is on active duty (or has been notified of an impending call or order to active duty). The Secretary of Labor has not issued final regulations regarding leave for any qualifying exigency. In the interim, employers are not required to comply in providing the appropriate leave, but are encouraged to do so. As such leave amends the FLMA, FMLA type procedures should be used as may be appropriate.

A detailed guide to FMLA as well as an update on the guidance regarding the new legislation can be found at http://www.dol.gov/esa/whd/fmla/index.htm.

The Paul Wellstone and Pete Domenici Mental Health Parity and Addiction Equity Act of 2008

Behavioral health parity legislation was signed into law on October 3, 2008, as part of the $700 billion financial rescue package. The measure requires that employers that provide health insurance plans cover mental health and addiction on the same basis as physical conditions. These provisions go into effect one year after enactment (October 8, 2009). At the time of this writing, the provisions are signed but not yet effective.

The mental health and addictions law:

- Applies to group health plans of 51 or more employees.
- Forbids employers and insurers from placing stricter limits on mental health and addictions care than on other health conditions.
- Applies to out-of-network coverage so that plans that provide network coverage must also provide such coverage for mental health conditions.
- Leaves in place and existing State parity measures.
- Requires that the US Departments of Labor, Health and Human Services and Treasury issue regulations within one year of enactment.

APPENDIX B. STEERING COMMITTEE MEMBERS

Melissa Auerbach
Attorney at Law
Cornfield and Feldman

Leslie Balonick
Regional Vice President
Westcare

Maria Canfield
Health Bureau Chief
Department of Health and Human Services
State of Nevada
Barbara Cimaglio

Dr. Janet H. Lenard
Clinical Director, Army
Substance Abuse Program
Southeast Regional ASAP
Coordinator
United States Army

Cynthia Moreno Tuohy
Executive Director
The Association for Addiction
Professionals (NAADAC)

Mark Sanders
Owner

Deputy Commissioner
Division of Alcohol and Drug Abuse
Programs
Vermont Dept. of Health

Dr. Seth Eisenberg
Director, Division of Addiction
Psychiatry and Addiction Psychiatry
Training Program
Northwestern Memorial Hospital

Judith Jobe
Vice President
Rosecrance Health Network

On the Mark Consulting

John Stuart
Vice President- Marketing
Better Business Planning

Becky Vaughn
Executive Director
State Associations of Addiction
Services

Andi Yakovitz
Account Executive
Bensinger, DuPont & Associates

In: Substance Use, Misuse and Relapse ...   ISBN: 978-1-62808-646-1
Editor: Jonas Eisenstadt   © 2013 Nova Science Publishers, Inc.

Chapter 2

SELF CARE: A GUIDE
FOR ADDICTION PROFESSIONALS[*]

Paula Jones, Aaron M. Williams and Glenda Clare

PURPOSE OF THE SELF-CARE GUIDE

The goal of this guide is to identify workplace stressors for addiction professionals and provide strategies for both agencies and addiction professionals that can be used to address these stressors and promote self-care. Both agencies and employees have a role to play in this process. While agencies can take steps to reduce workplace stress and provide opportunities to enhance the health and well-being of their employees, it is ultimately the responsibility of employees to take the steps necessary to adopt a healthier lifestyle and engage in activities that promote well being.

It is important to note that the suggestions in this guide are just that, suggestions. Every agency and individual has different needs and resources. No single approach is right for all agencies and individuals. Many of the suggested approaches are highly adaptable, allowing agencies and employees to select those aspects of an approach that best meet their needs.

It is also important to emphasize that there may be some situations in the workplace, such as funding cuts, new regulations, or increased demand for

---

[*] This is an edited, reformatted and augmented version of the Central East Addiction Technology Transfer Center, dated October 2011.

services, over which agencies and employees have little or no control. While little can be done to address these situations, some of the strategies suggested in the guide will help employees better adapt to emerging situations and minimize the negative impact on their professional performance and personal life.

SECTION I. CHALLENGES IN THE WORKPLACE

Goal of Section:
Identify work-related factors that can impact well-being

Why Is the Workplace Stressful?

All work environments can have stressful aspects. Since for most of us, work is not an option but a necessity, most people cannot avoid the stress that they experience at work. Common stressors that all employees experience, no matter what the job or work environment, are listed below.

Relationships with Management

Even a good manager sometimes makes mistakes, and a bad manager can make many mistakes. Managers can create stress in the workplace through poor management practices such as failing to provide appropriate supervision, providing unclear or no guidance on expected job performance, failing to establish and maintain the necessary processes and procedures, and by showing favoritism. Even if a manager has strong management skills, he or she may lack the necessary interpersonal or "people" skills that are essential to a well-run workplace.

Relationships with Co-workers

Dealing with the many personalities that populate the workplace can create stress. As adults, many of us hope that the schoolyard antics from our younger years are far behind us. Unfortunately, many of the unpleasant characters from our past, the bully, gossip, and tattletale, show up in the workplace. There are also other characters, such as "the slacker" and people who take credit for the work of others that are unique to the workplace. In addition, there can be personality conflicts between employees that are not related to job performance; some people just don't get along. While it is important to be professional and treat co-workers in a professional manner, dealing with the multiple personalities that make up the workplace can create stress.

Bureaucracy/Red Tape

In most jobs there are certain ways that things must be done. Some of these procedures and processes make sense and increase efficiency, others may seem designed to complicate and lengthen the workday. Sometimes employees have no input into how things are run, but more and more employers are listening to employees' suggestions about how to reduce bureaucracy and increase efficiency.

Performance Demands

We go to work to work, and while at work, we are expected to perform to a certain standard. Sometimes, these standards can be impossible to achieve, either because they are set too high or due to other circumstances. These circumstances can relate to the workplace, such as staffing changes, changes in processes and procedures, or changes in caseloads, or they can relate to individuals such as illness or personal problems that impact an employee's ability to do his or her job. Setting standards too low can also create problems. Not having enough work to do and low expectations on the part of management can significantly undermine productivity and create an unpleasant work environment.

Balancing Professional and Personal Life

We spend a significant amount of our time at work, making it easy for jobs to overlap with personal lives. This can have a huge impact on health and personal relationships. Learning to "leave work at work" and not take it home is important to maintaining a balance between the two.

What Additional Challenges Confront Addiction Professionals?

Addiction professionals face many challenges in their work that go beyond those previously stated. If strategies to address these challenges are not adopted at the agency and individual levels, significant stress, as well as other problems, can result.

Challenging Patient Population

Our clients have very complex, and sometimes overwhelming, lives. In addition to their addictions, they are often dealing with medical, legal, family, housing, and employment issues. Our job is to help our clients. Sometimes, it is possible to get overly involved in the needs of clients or overwhelmed trying to help a large number of extremely needy individuals. This can result in "burnout" or secondary stress disorder which is more commonly referred to as "compassion fatigue" (Figley, 1985).

Agencies Often Lack Adequate Resources

Addiction treatment agencies come in all shapes and sizes. Some are small community-based organizations; others are operated by State and local governments. Because of the demand for services, many of these providers, whether from the public sector or private sector, have extremely tight budgets. This can impact the work environment in terms of large caseloads, low levels of compensation, and the ability of organizations to implement measures to support staff in their work (McLellan, Carise, & Kleber 2003).

Lack of a Clear Career Path for Addiction Professionals

For many addiction professionals, it is unclear what steps they must take to advance in the profession. Some providers require specific licenses and credentials, while others hire people with significant experience on the street dealing with the target population. It is not uncommon for people to work their way up from volunteer positions to those with more responsibility. However, employees with significant experience sometimes get passed over for promotion in favor of those with higher degrees (Hoge et al., 2005).

This lack of a clear career path can lead to frustration and a lack of motivation among addiction professionals. Standardized positions and uniform requirements would help those working in this profession understand what steps are necessary to attain specific positions. With clearer guidance, more addiction professionals may be motivated to seek additional education and training (U.S. Department of Health and Human Services, 2006).

Recovery Management

Many addiction professionals come to the field as a result of their own experience with addiction. According to a National Treatment Center Study released in 1999, which surveyed counselors in 400 treatment programs, roughly 60 percent of addiction counselors were in recovery (CSAT, 2006). This personal perspective can result in insight and empathy. However, it can also put those in recovery at risk of relapse. Every day, they deal with people who are struggling with addiction. Addiction professionals who are in recovery must be mindful of the risks and take appropriate steps to maintain their recovery. Working as an addiction professional does not constitute a personal plan of recovery.

Health Issues

Because of the nature of addiction there is a high rate of co-morbidity with other chronic conditions, such as depression, HIV/AIDS and hepatitis (CSAT, 1995). Professionals who are also in recovery may be dealing with these or other chronic diseases and infections as a result of their drug use. Most of these chronic diseases are manageable but may impact an individual's ability to perform their professional duties. Such conditions require regular, ongoing medical management, necessitating time off the job for medical appointments. Tensions can arise as employees who are not confronted by such health issues are repeatedly asked to step in for their colleagues who must take time off. In addition, staff may suffer from conditions that are totally unrelated to prior addictions, such as asthma, diabetes, or high blood pressure, which also require accommodation.

High Burnout and Turnover Rates

Due to the various factors identified above, addiction professionals have very high turnover rates, an estimated 50 percent in some agencies (McLellan, Carise, & Kleber, 2003).

Therapists and counselors are highly susceptible to burnout and compassion fatigue due to some aspects of the job, such as the drain of remaining empathy and the high rate of relapse among clients. At times, success stories can be few and far between. This draining of empathy can limit the addiction professional's ability to help clients and effect treatment outcome (Rothschild & Rand, 2006).

Burnout and turnover can result in an endless cycle in the workplace: employees burn out due to work-related stresses; burnt-out employees seek other employment; and remaining employees face even higher caseloads, which creates even more work-related stress (IOM, 2004). To break this cycle, agencies and employees must address the work-related stress that may be the root cause of burnout.

Boundaries

Employees need a clear understanding of boundaries to do their jobs effectively and reduce the possibility of inappropriate client interactions and the stress resulting from such interactions. There are various types of boundaries that must be established and maintained. Employees need to know how much of themselves they can give to clients and the extent to which they can help them. Burnout can result from a lack of appropriate boundaries (Rothschild & Rand, 2006).

Employees also require training on how to deal with certain situations that may occur. For example, counselors, especially those working in smaller communities, may encounter clients outside of work. Agencies need to prepare staff for these encounters. For confidentiality reasons, staff should not initiate interactions with clients. However, if clients initiate encounters, employees could engage with the client, if they felt it was appropriate. Employees should be provided certain strategies, such as suggesting that the client call them the next workday if they need assistance. Such a strategy allows employee to maintain thir personal time while still addressing the needs of the client.

It is important to remember that boundaries are two-sided. Employees must understand that they should not overstep the clients' boundaries, but they must also be aware that they need to protect themselves and make sure that their own personal boundaries are maintained.

Professional/Ethical Standards

Most professions, such as physicians, journalists, and lawyers, have a specific professional code of ethics, which provides standards of behavior and principles related to moral and professional obligations. Codes guide the conduct of professionals in their interactions with clients, colleagues, and society in general. These codes are generally developed by professional societies. For example, NAADAC, the National Association of Addiction Professionals has a code of ethics that address nine principles:

1) Non-discrimination
2) Client welfare
3) Client relationships
4) Trustworthiness
5) Compliance with law
6) Rights and duties
7) Dual relationships

8) Preventing harm
9) Duty to Care.

Source: www.naadac.org

Many of the challenges in the workplace are related to a violation of ethical standards. Some of these are intentional, but often, staff have not received training on what constitutes inappropriate and unprofessional behavior.

SECTION II. AGENCY ROLE IN SUPPORTING WELL-BEING

Goal of Section:

Identify ways agencies can reduce stress in the workplace and support well-being of employees

There are many benefits to promoting well-being in the workplace. Employees who are physically and mentally healthy are often more productive, perform better, and are absent less often than other employees (Aldana, 2001). This can result in better performance for the agency, better services for clients, and a less stressful and more supportive work environment for employees.

Creating a healthy, supportive, productive work environment is the responsibility of both employers and employees. One cannot do it without the help and cooperation of the other. Agencies and employees should work together on an ongoing basis to promote the well-being of all employees. The key to this process is communication and a willingness to listen. Strategies can be as simple as the old-fashioned suggestion box or more formal, such as an employee advisory committee.

The efforts of agencies to promote well-being in the workplace should focus on all staff, not just counselors. All employees, including receptionists, compliance technicians, nurses and physicians, and outreach workers can benefit from programs to promote well-being.

Organizationally, an agency must be prepared to support employees. Once an agency's staff begins to grow beyond a certain point, qualified, competent human resources professionals should be employed. These professionals are trained to address and resolve various issues within the workplace such as job satisfaction, motivation, and commitment. Human resources professionals should receive ongoing training and have access to various tools and resources that can help them continually enhance the work environment.

Agencies should also not overlook the physical aspects of the work-place. To the extent possible, agencies should endeavor to create a comfortable work environment with comfortable furniture, good lighting, and adequate work and meeting space. If possible, amenities such as a quiet room, kitchen, and shower/changing facilities should be made available.

All agencies are different and have different resources and needs. No single approach will work in all workplaces. However, there are gen-eral approaches that agencies can implement.

1. Flexibility

Conforming to a rigid schedule can create significant stress in employees' lives as they try to address personal needs related to their health, recovery, and family responsibilities or pursue additional education. Allowing flexibility in scheduling, such as multiple-shift options or flexibility in terms of when employees start and finish their workdays, allows employees to fit in medical appointments, AA or NA meetings, or pick up a child from daycare. Similarly, some flexibility during the workday, such as when employees take lunch, can also provide time for employees to address their personal needs, such as going to the gym. The degree to which agencies can allow employees flexibility in their schedules will vary. Adopting a "flex-time" policy that adjusts but does not reduce the hours worked may be the most feasible to implement. It is important to note that some employees may take advantage of this increased flexibility. Processes should be in place to ensure that all employees put in a full workday. Whatever the policy, it should be clearly stated so staff are aware of what is and is not acceptable.

2. Appropriate Supervision

Supervision is not simply a mechanism for determining whether employees are performing their jobs. Research suggests that in addition to providing an ongoing evaluation of skills, appropriate clinical supervision can reduce staff stress and increase motivation (Powell & Brodsky, 2004).

Supervisors should be both well-trained in supervisory techniques and have the time necessary to supervise staff adequately. Both individual and group supervision should occur regularly.

Employees need regular, consistent feedback on both clinical and other work-related issues. This process should be both formal, with regularly scheduled sessions, and informal. Informal check-ins can take many forms. For example, supervisors may make a point of checking in with all staff at the end of the day when people are saying goodnight and preparing to go home. Supervisors should also watch their employees for signs that may indicate personal or health-related problems such as mood swings, weight gain or loss, tardiness, and absenteeism.

PROVIDING CATCH-UP TIME

It is easy to get behind with paperwork and have things start piling up on the desk. It can be very hard to tackle this backlog during the course of a normal work day. While it may sound contradictory to supporting staff, some employees prefer to catch up by working on the weekend a couple times a year. This allows them to focus on the work without interruptions. Employers may want to consider setting up a policy allowing employees to do this and granting them a day off during their normal work week to compensate them for coming in over the weekend.

For addiction professionals, research suggests that it is important that supervisors also address the following:

- Relationships between recovering staff and clients
- Professional credibility
- Cultural bias and unfair treatment
- Staff performance evaluations
- Liability concerns
- Impaired counselors (CSAT, 2006)

3. Professional Development

Agencies should encourage employees to pursue opportunities to build their skills and enhance their careers. Employees should receive training on professional and ethical standards so that they have an understanding of the agency's expectations concerning professional conduct. Agencies should also foster an environment that encourages professional growth. Some agencies may have the resources to help employees pursue additional education by providing tuition reimbursement and additional time off to attend classes.

Not all employees will want or need to pursue additional education but can still benefit from learning new skills. Agencies can provide in-service training or continuing education opportunities. Employees can also attend outside trainings and conferences and bring these skills back to other employees through presentations and in-house trainings. On-the-job training, such as assigning new responsibilities (with appropriate supervision), can also empower employees and help them grow professionally.

4. Professional and Ethical Standards

Agencies should develop their own rules of conduct, provide appropriate training to staff, and ensure that these rules are universally observed and enforced.

Traits Addiction Professionals Should Exhibit

- Familiarity with mandatory reporting requirements
- Adherence to professional standards and scope of practice
- Knowledge of the difference between a clinical relationship and that of a peer counselor or sponsor to a client
- Willingness to use clinical supervision and peer assessments to gain insights into clinical performance, especially deficiencies
- Awareness of current research and trends in addiction and related fields
- Involvement in professional organizations
- Respect for clients from diverse backgrounds
- Recognition of the effect that personal bias toward other cultures and lifestyles can have on treatment
- Understanding of personal recovery and its effect on the provision of treatment
- Capacity to conduct self evaluation
- Participation in regular continuing education
- Use of self-care strategies

Source: SAMHSA, CSAT, Treatment Improvement Protocol (TIP) 46, Substance Abuse: Administrative Issues in Outpatient Treatment

Minimum Professional and Ethical Responsibilities for Addiction Professionals

- Adhere to established professional codes of ethics that define the professional context within which the counselor works in order to maintain professional standards and safeguard the client.
- Adhere to Federal and State laws and agency regulations regarding the treatment of substance use disorders.
- Interpret and apply information from current counseling and psychoactive substance use research literature to improve client care and enhance professional growth.
- Recognize the importance of individual differences that influence client behavior and apply this understanding to clinical practice.
- Utilize a range of supervisory options to process personal feelings and concerns about clients.
- Conduct self-evaluations of professional performance applying ethical, legal, and professional standards to enhance self-awareness and performance.
- Obtain appropriate continuing professional education.
- Participate in ongoing supervision and consultation.
- Develop and utilize strategies to maintain one's own physical and mental health.

Source: SAMHSA, CSAT Technical Assistance Publication (TAP) 21: Addiction Counseling Competencies: The Knowledge, Skills, and Attitudes of Professional Practice

5. Encourage Well-Being in the Workplace

Agencies can play an important role in encouraging and facilitating self-care. Part of this is creating an organizational culture that values and promotes self-care. There are also concrete things agencies can do. For example, to encourage employees to eat right, agencies can provide information and training on nutrition and provide healthy snacks at work-related events. Agencies can provide bottle water throughout the office to make sure employees stay well hydrated. To encourage exercise, agencies can subsidize gym memberships, pay initiation fees, obtain group rates, or provide on-site opportunities for exercise such as yoga classes or walking programs. Agencies can also provide information to employees or hold in-service training on activities that promote mental wellness such as meditation, relaxation techniques, and stress-reduction techniques such as journaling.

Many agencies have employee assistance programs in place that provide employees access to mental health and other support services. Agencies can also offer activities that provide "mental health breaks" to employees such as the following:

CREATING A CULTURE OF WELLNESS

- Maintain a Strong Commitment to Well-Being. Have a genuine interest in employees and an ongoing commitment to their well-being.
- Provide Information. Employees need information on their options when it comes to self-care. In addition to making information available, management and supervisors should foster resourcefulness on the part of employees and empower employees to address their own needs.
- Provide Role Models. Management and supervisors should model healthy behaviors. The agency should create a culture of wellness from the top down.
- Respond to Stressful Events. Agencies should be mindful of events that increase stress in the workplace and be prepared to provide additional support to employees. For example, the death of a fellow employee or a client should be acknowledged and support provided to help employees mourn such losses. Agencies should also consider building in support activities in relation to specific events, such as HIV testing initiatives when employees will be giving out a large number of test results in a very short period of time. Opportunities to discuss what happened and decompress should be built into the process.

Retreats

Many agencies hold annual (or more frequent) retreats for their employees. These retreats are designed to give employees a chance to relax, rejuvenate, and develop skills that promote mental wellness (see Sample Retreat Agenda in Appendix).

Special Events

Agencies plan a variety of special events for employees that allow them to "blow off steam" and enjoy each others' company in a non-work-related environment. These activities include outings such as picnics and bowling. Even onsite events, such as birthday parties, can significantly boost staff morale.

6. Support Staff in Recovery

Supporting staff in recovery can play a critial role in maintaining staff motivation and morale. The degree to which agencies can support their employees in recovery varies. Some agencies chose to incorporate recovery into their general wellness-related activities instead of having separate activities and programs for employees in recovery. Other agencies may hold support groups on site or provide opportunities for staff to attend AA or NA meetings.

Agencies should have a policy in place about the length of time counselors must be in recovery before being hired. People who have been in recovery for less than a year are generally not hired for counseling positions. However, non-counseling or volunteer positions may be appropriate for people in early recovery (CSAT, 2006).

LAWS RELATING TO THE HIRING OF STAFF IN RECOVERY

There are two Federal laws that protect certain individuals with substance use disorders from discrimination in employment. These are:

- Federal Rehabilitation Act (29 United States Code [U.S.C.] 791 et seq. [1973])
- Americans with Disabilities Act (ADA) (42 U.S.C. 12101 et seq. [1992]).

These laws protect people with a history of substance use disorders, some people who currently abuse substances, and people who are receiving treatment. There are also laws in some States that protect people who formerly and/or currently abuse substances. Not all programs are subject to these laws.

In general, the laws:

- Regard people with substance use disorders as individuals with disabilities but distinguish between individuals who are in recovery and those who currently abuse substances and between alcohol abuse and illegal drug abuse
- Protect people who abused alcohol and drugs in the past and are in recovery
- Provide limited protection against employment discrimination to people who currently abuse alcohol but who can perform the requisite job duties and do not pose a direct threat to the health, safety, or property of others in the workplace
- Do not protect people currently abusing illegal drugs, even if they are qualified and do not pose a direct threat to others in the workplace
- Protect people who are participating in a supervised rehabilitation program and no longer are engaged in drug or alcohol abuse
- Protect only those people that are qualified for employment (i.e., an individual who, with or without reasonable accommodation, can perform the essential functions of the employment position)

In addition, the laws prohibit the use of standards or other selection criteria that screen out individuals with a disability unless these standards or criteria are shown to be job related and necessary for conducting business. The laws also prohibit pre-employment medical examinations or inquiries about applicants' disabilities unless it is shown to be job-related and consistent with the needs of the business.

Federal laws can change and State laws can vary. Agencies should take steps to make sure their policies and practices are in accordance with existing laws through their human resources department or by consulting legal counsel.

Source: SAMHSA, CSAT, Treatment Improvement Protocol (TIP) 46, Substance Abuse: Administrative Issues in Outpatient Treatment.

SECTION III. SELF-CARE APPROACHES

Goal of Section:
Identify some of the self-care approaches that employees can use to increase their own well-being

This section identifies specific areas where employees can take steps to improve their well-being. Eating better, regular exercise, and taking steps to enhance mental well-being can all have a significant impact on overall health and personal outlook. There is also a lot of overlap across the topics identified below. For example, regular exercise can reduce stress, which increases mental wellness. Exercise can also address some of the negative impacts of an unhealthy diet (if you can not change it). Finding a balance is important.

The areas identified below are good places to start. However, they are not the only ways to increase well-being. Personal happiness and well-being can be derived from various sources, whether it is a hobby, quality time with family or a significant other, or a rewarding volunteer commitment. This guide is designed to get you started in the right direction, but you should not limit your self-care efforts to the suggestions in this guide.

Agencies can certainly play a role in supporting self-care. The degree to which agencies can do this depends on their resources. Responses can vary from providing information on community resources to providing significant in-house support. Agencies can take steps to help employees increase their well-being but ultimately, it is up to the individual to decide the extent to which they will take advantage of these opportunities.

Topics

- Nutrition[*]
- Exercise/Health Promotion[*]
- Mental Wellness
- Recovery Management

---

[*] The information contained in this section, particularly as it relates to Nutrition and Exercise are suggestions based on current research and discussion with Central East ATTCs' Advisory Panel. This information should not be used as a substitute for the opinions of trained medical professionals. Before changing any diet or exercise routine it is recommended that you consult a medical professional.

1. Nutrition

A healthy diet is one that provides enough of each essential nutrient, contains a variety of foods from all of the basic food groups, provides adequate energy, and does not contain excess fat, sugar, and salt.

There are many reasons maintain a healthy diet. These include:

- Improved health
- Increased energy
- Managing weight gain
- Preventing and managing diseases and disorders

There is an obesity epidemic in the United States. Results from the 2005–2006 National Health and Nutrition Examination Survey (NHANES) show that an estimated one-third of U.S. adults are either overweight or obese. This includes 33.3% men and 33.8% of women now being considered obese. This epidemic is attributed to the overconsumption of high-calorie food and a sedentary lifestyle (CDC, 2006).

Even though eating healthy food can make us feel better, it is not always easy. Sometimes it seems much easier to grab a quick meal at a fast food restaurant instead of packing a healthy lunch at home. It can also be hard to say no when your co-workers are indulging in unhealthy snacks. It is important to remember that even little changes in diet can make a difference and big changes can make a big difference. Below are steps you can take to improve your diet.

HOW DOES HEALTHY EATING HELP ADDICTION PROFESSIONALS?

Today, we live in a fast-paced world where everything must happen "now". The addictions field is no different. Customers come into treatment on a voluntary or mandated basis. They come with the expectation that "I am going to be fixed now."

The program staff wants to help, but oftentimes are burdened with their own addictions, stress, or physical problems. Many of these issues can be helped through healthy life choices, continuing education, accepting that they can help a person only when that person is ready, and monitoring their own health.

On any given day across this country, one can observe an addiction professional standing in front of a facility smoking a cigarette, drinking a cup of coffee, soda or eating an unhealthy snack. Many eat sugary treats and high-calorie foods with little nutritional value throughout the day and before the day is over, they are too tired to provide services effectively. They are irritable, tired, and not focused on the needs of the customers. This, in my opinion, causes stress, burnout, and numerous health problems that can be prevented through healthy eating and lifestyle changes. In my conversations with addiction practitioners many have stated that they have health problems (high blood pressure, high cholesterol, diabetes, gout, severe arthritis, headaches, hair loss, and chronic fatigue syndrome).

This brought me to the conclusion that food plays a major role in how we do our jobs and treat our customers. Here are some suggestions on what I believe, through research and my personal experiences with food and changing my own lifestyle, can help other addiction professionals:

- Limit or eliminate all caffeinated drinks (coffee, tea, sodas, energy drinks) during the work day
    - Drink more water, fruit juices, health drinks, decaffeinated tea
- Cut down or eliminate sugary snacks (donuts/pastries, cakes, pies, candy individual pieces and bars, salty snacks)
    - Eat healthy snacks: sliced vegetables, fruit (fresh/dried), granola, fiber, fruit bars, salt-free snacks and nuts
- Eliminate eating fast-food
- Monitor food portions throughout the day:
    - Morning: bottled water, bowl of cereal, cup of fruit or yogurt, breakfast sandwich, bagel, protein or fruit drink or granola bar
    - Mid-day snack: bottled water, piece of fruit, granola/health bar
    - Lunch: bottled water, fruit/vegetable plate, fresh green salad with fresh vegetables or tuna/chicken, sandwich (meat of choice) on multi-grain bread with greens, piece of fruit, healthy snack, protein drink, or light portion control frozen meals

> - Mid-afternoon snack: bottle of water, piece of fruit, granola health bar, salt-free snack
> - Decrease or eliminate smoking and alcohol intake
> - Take a walk outside of your office or around the block during the day. The fresh air will stimulate oxygen and help increase energy to maintain workload
>
> Valerie E. Robinson, MS, LPC Consultant, The Danya Institute

Learn about Nutrition

There are lots of ways to learn about healthy eating. Information is available from books and websites. For those who prefer to learn through classes, many are available. Many organizations offer classes on nutrition, healthy eating, and food preparation.

Don't Get Overwhelmed

There are literally thousands of diets and approaches to weight loss, just look on the Best Sellers list or a magazine rack and you will be confronted with 10 to 20 of the latest diets. Before starting a diet, be sure to research your options and consider discussing it with your physician. Consider various aspects of the diet, such as whether it will require you to prepare special foods in addition to the food you prepare for your family and the cost of the food the diet recommends. Also, the length of time you will be on the diet is a consideration. Consider whether you will stick to the diet for 30 days, 3 months, or 6 months. If the diet is not right for your lifestyle, it can be very hard to maintain.

Consider What You are Eating

Get in the habit of reading labels and looking at the nutritional information on packages. Many restaurants also make nutritional information available. Knowing what you are eating can help you make healthy choices.

Portion Size

In addition to watching what you eat, you need to watch how much you eat. America's obesity epidemic has been attributed not only to what we are eating but how much we are eating. United States Department of Agriculture (USDA) statistics indicate that the total daily caloric intake for Americans has risen from 1,854 to 2,002 calories over the last 20 years. This increase, 148 calories per day, works out to an extra 15 pounds every year (DHHS/USDA,

2005). Techniques for limiting portion size include weighing your food, checking the serving sizes on packages, and avoiding "Super Sizing."

DON'T FORGET WATER

Keeping the body well hydrated can have a significant impact on health. Almost two-thirds of our body weight is water. Water is necessary to digest food and absorb vitamins and nutrients. It plays a role in detoxifying the liver and kidneys and removing waste and toxins from the body. If you are dehydrated, the body must work harder to circulate the blood, leaving you less energy to do the things you want and need to do.

How much water should you drink? The general rule is eight 8-ounce glasses of water a day. Another way to determine how many ounces of water you should drink a day is to divide your weight by two. For example, if you weigh 150 pounds you should drink 75 ounces of water a day (150 divided by 2 is 75).

Tips for Staying Hydrated

- Avoid drinking liquids such as coffee, tea, or soda, which often contain caffeine. These can actually result in the loss of water from the body since caffeine is a diuretic.
- When you are exercising remember to drink plenty of water before, during, and after to compensate for the water that you may lose through perspiration.
- Drink before you feel thirsty. You are already dehydrated when you feel thirsty.
- Keep a bottle of water with you at all times.
- Make water available in places were you spend a significant amount of your time, like work. Consider setting up a water club at the office and sharing the cost of having bottled water delivered.

Plan to Eat Right

Eating right doesn't just happen, you need to plan for it. This can take the form of taking your lunch to work or having healthy snacks, such as fruits, carrot sticks, or nuts, at your desk so you can avoid the temptation of buying a candy bar or soda. If you are going to an event where you know there will be unhealthy food, have a healthy snack before you arrive. It is much easier to resist temptation if you are not hungry.

Recruit Others to Eat Healthy

It is much easier to eat healthy foods if others around you are doing the same. Consider recruiting a friend or co-worker and motivate each other to make healthy nutritional choices. Encourage your employer to provide healthy snacks at meetings and work-related functions (or at least some healthy alternatives).

Get Help

Not everyone can change eating habits on their own. There are numerous programs available to help people adopt healthier eating habits. Some of these, such as Weight Watchers®, have fees associated with their services. Others are available at no cost.

Resources

American Dietetic Association

ADA's Knowledge Center provides timely and objective food and nutrition information.

TheDietChannel.com

A health, nutrition and weight loss resource that features links, and reviews of popular diet programs, as well as articles and other information on nutrition and weight loss.

Nutrition.Gov

A clearinghouse of U.S. Government information on food and nutrition. Includes information on weight management, shopping, cooking, meal planning, nutrition and health issues, and dietary supplements.

2. Exercise/Health Promotion

"Life belongs to God and health belongs to you!"

– Dr. Nan Lu

There are some aspects of our health over which we have no control, such as genetics and environment. However, there are many things that can be done to positively impact health and well-being. Exercise and other steps, like stopping smoking (see Smoking Cessation in Appendix), can significantly enhance overall health and prevent the development of health-related problems in the future.

An important aspect of wellness is to take the necessary steps to monitor your health. This includes regular physical exams and the recommended screenings for your age group (such as cholesterol screenings, mammograms, and prostate exams). By detecting health-related problems early, through regular physical exams, intervention can begin earlier and hopefully address problems before they become serious.

Physical activity has been shown to be the single most important factor in successful weight maintenance. In addition to limiting weight gain, exercise can reduce the risk of many serious health-related conditions, such as high blood pressure, heart disease, osteoporosis, and diabetes. Regular physical activity has also been shown to reduce anxiety and depression, and to improve mood.

In addition, the loss of strength and stamina often attributed to aging is partly caused by reduced physical activity. All of these benefits can translate into better performance on the job (as well as in one's personal life).

Getting Started

Physical Check Up

Before you begin any exercise regimen check with your doctor to make sure that your plans are appropriate and will not result in any complications.

Select the Right Activity

There are many different types of exercises: walking, running, biking, aerobics, swimming, and team sports. Choosing an activity you enjoy can greatly impact whether you stick with your exercise routine. Don't be afraid to try something new and consider incorporating more than one activity into your routine. Engaging in several activities makes things more interesting and can reduce the chance of injuries.

COMMON EXCUSES FOR NOT EXERCISING

- I don't have enough time.
- It's too hot (or too cold) outside.
- I have a health condition that keeps me from exercising.
- I'm too old to start exercising.
- I don't have the right shoes and clothing.
- I don't enjoy it.
- It's too boring.
- It leaves me too tired to do the things I need to do.
- It takes time away from my family.

Start Slow

Plan to start slowly and gradually build up over time, especially if you have not exercised for a while. Injury can result if you try to start too fast.

Keep it Interesting

Some people thrive on the same routine but for many, doing the same thing every time can get boring. Explore ways to keep your exercise routine interesting. For example, find a workout partner or bring your favorite music to the gym.

Resources

The President's Council on Physical Fitness and Sports

The web site includes links to the resources of government agencies as well as to health and fitness organizations.

Physical Fitness is for Everyone

This CDC fact sheet includes: tips for being more active; risks to being active; tips for avoiding activity-induced injuries; and information on overcoming barriers to physical activity.

Shape Up America!

Shape Up America! is committed to raising awareness of obesity as a health issue and providing responsible information on healthy weight management. The web site includes numerous resources and assessments to help people determine readiness for physical activity, overcome common barriers to physical activity, and design a fitness plan.

3. Mental Wellness

"Helpers have a hard time asking for help. You cannot continue to give unless you receive."

– LaShaun Evans

Addiction professionals work in a demanding and stressful environment, and in order to provide optimal services to clients, they must be mentally healthy. Counselors or outreach workers who are struggling with stress or depression may be unable to respond to their clients needs, and in this line of work, that can have serious repercussions. Therefore, it is imperative that addiction professionals develop a regimen of self-care that promotes mental wellness.

Everyone should be taking steps to promote mental wellness. We live in a very stressful society, and addiction professionals have stressful jobs. There are also other factors that can impact mental well-being.

The National Institute of Mental Health (NIMH) reports that an estimated 26.2 percent of Americans, ages 18 and older, approximately one in four adults, suffer from a diagnosable mental disorder in a given year (NIMH, 2007). While mental disorders are fairly widespread in the population, a much smaller proportion of the population, about 6 percent, suffer from a serious mental illness. Mental disorders are the leading cause of disability in the United States. Just because you are a behavioral health professional doesn't mean you are immune from mental health disorders.

MAKE HEALTHY DECISIONS

Regular Check Up

Even if you feel healthy, do not neglect to see your doctor for regular check ups. Be sure that you receive the screenings recommended for your age.

Take your Medications

If you are on medications for a chronic condition such as HIV disease, hepatitis, diabetes, or high blood pressure, be sure to take your medication regularly and not skip doses.

Stay Home when Sick

For various reasons, people still come to work when they are sick. This can compromise your own health and also put put the health of clients and co-workers at risk. If you are sick, seek appropriate care and stay home until you recover.

Infectious Disease Precautions

Some clients may have infectious diseases, such as HIV, hepatitis, and tuberculosis (TB). Employees should always use universal precautions.

It is crucial to know the signs that indicate you may need help from a mental health professional. In particular, if you have thoughts about hurting yourself or someone else, you should seek care from a mental health professional. Other key signs include symptoms that:

- Disrupt performance of regular activities
- Become markedly more severe
- Become a regular pattern instead of an intermittent occurrence
- Increase in number

MAINTAINING BOUNDARIES

The patients we work with almost always lack boundaries, usually specific to histories of abuse, family of origin and life experiences in their addiction. To maintain a healthy but therapeutic (helpful) relationship with clients, professionals in the field of addiction need to maintain their own boundaries as well.

We have always heard: "that person will push your buttons." When this happens it is due to a lack of boundaries or unresolved issues on the part of the professional. Clients cannot push buttons that are healed and not obvious to them.

Most human beings' unresolved issues stem from life experiences and clients may pick up on these. Many individuals working in the field of addiction are recovering themselves.

Being in recovery can help professionals empathize with the client; however it can also cause problems in the therapeutic relationship if the professionals have unresolved issues related to their own addiction.

Addiction professionals are more effective maintaining boundaries when they have resolved or are working on their own issues. Picture us with a shield all around us. The shield has "holes" which are our issues. The more they are resolved, the smaller the holes in which clients can get through and push our buttons. More importantly, the smaller these holes the healthier the employee will be maintaining boundaries with the client. When these holes are not resolved or maintained at a healthy level, we will almost always invade the clients' boundaries.

The most important point to all of this is the fact that we are all human beings on a life road of growing and learning.

Take notice of specific areas where you feel you have invaded a client's boundaries and the areas in which clients continue to "push our buttons" and there you will find the areas in which you need a little more growth.

Walter Williams
Executive Director, Synergy Treatment Centers, Inc.

While there is no substitute for treatment for a diagnosed (or undiagnosed) mental disorder, because of the nature of the work, addiction professionals should employ specific strategies to enhance mental well-being.

- **Set Boundaries**
  As discussed earlier, it is essential to maintain boundaries in interactions with clients. These boundaries must apply to the level of emotional engagement, professional ethics, and interactions with clients outside of the workplace. Failure to observe these boundaries can create significant job-related stress, severely impact professional performance, and compromise the quality of care provided to clients.
- **Conduct Regular Self-Assessments**[*]
  How am I doing? Employees should regularly check in with themselves to assess their mental well-being. Because of the stressful, fast-paced environment, it is easy to overlook things that need to be acknowledged. Self-assessments can help employees to step back and

[*] Examples of stress self-assessment tools can be found in the Appendix.

grieve a loss or celebrate an accomplishment that may have otherwise been overlooked. It can also help employees keep tabs on their overall self-care efforts and ask questions like, "Am I taking the office home with me?" "Am I eating right?" or "Have I been letting the boundaries with clients slip?"

- **Create Personal Rituals**
  Some counselors rely on personal rituals to help clear their minds and refocus their thoughts. These rituals can be performed at the start of the day, between client visits, or at the end of the day. For example, one visualization technique some counselors perform between clients is to imagine they are enclosed in a bubble. The positive energy from the counselor can travel through the bubble to the client. However, any negative energy from the client is stopped by the bubble. Others have a specific ritual for the end of the day, such as making a "To Do" list for the next day, to help ensure that work is left at the office and not brought home.
- **Take a "Mental Health" Break between Clients**
  Whether you are performing a specific ritual or just taking a break, try to take a few minutes between clients, to decompress, relax, and refocus.
- **Learn to Relax**
  While at one time it may have been an innate skill, many of us have long since forgotten how to relax. Fortunately, it is possible to relearn this skill. Various exercises, centered around meditation, grounding, and muscle relaxation, can greatly enhance mental wellness. Increased ability to relax will have multiple benefits, including improved sleep and better physical health.
- **Conduct Your Own Personal Retreats**
  You don't have to wait for your agency to hold a retreat. In many communities there are non-profit organizations that offer activities designed for rejuvenation. Some of these organizations have a spiritual focus. Even if you cannot find an organization that offers individual retreats, consider planning your own, perhaps a massage, hiking in the woods, or reading an inspirational book.
- **Make Time Outside of Work**
  Modern life is increasingly busy. Just because you are off work doesn't mean you are relaxing; you may be doing your "other" job of taking care of family and personal responsibilities. Schedule times to

do things you enjoy, whether it is dinner out in a restaurant and a movie, an art class, book group, or regular exercise.

THE IMPORTANCE OF SPIRITUALITY

Spirituality has been generally defined as a "search for the sacred," and typically emphasizes the boundaries of human material existence (Miller, 1998). However, spirituality can mean different things to different people and it is not easy to define for most.

For the purposes of this guide, we will not attempt to define it. What can be said is that spirituality is intensely personal. It is also, many will argue, crucial to well-being.

Key elements of spirituality may include:

- Development of greater self-awareness
- Seeking out interconnectedness
- A relationship with a higher power

Some people choose to take an individualized approach to spirituality while others seek out the fellowship of others.

As for recognizing spirituality in the workplace, the key words are tolerance and diversity, celebrating spirituality within different cultures, religions, and traditions. Some agencies have explored spirituality by planning presentations on various religions such as Buddhism, Christianity, Hinduism, Islam, Judaism, etc. Such presentations help demystify religions and can help employees focus on the common elements that all religions share.

Agencies should also ask employees to help identify their spiritual needs. Involving employees in this process can help agencies better meet the spiritual needs of employees in the workplace. For example, employees may request that space be dedicated for a quiet room, which could be used for meditation and prayer during the day.

Recommended readings on spirituality:

The Spirituality of Imperfection, Storytelling and Journey to Wholeness, by Ernest Kurtz and Katherine Ketcham
Care of the Soul, A Guide for Cultivating Depth and Sacredness in Everyday Life, by Thomas Moore

- **Build a Support Network with Fellow Employees**
  Some people find it helpful to maintain close relationships with one or two co-workers who provide support, feedback, as well as a regular opportunity to check in on issues related to professional integrity.

DEALING WITH STRESS

As discussed earlier, addiction professionals experience many stressors in the workplace. In addition to job-related stress, stress can also be generated from circumstances in our personal lives.

Stress can be brief and highly situational or it can be more persistent. Stress can become a serious problem if it begins to interfere with normal activities and lasts for an extended period. High levels of stress can result in fatigue, inability to concentrate, and irritability.

It is possible to manage stress. The following steps can help reduce the level of stress in your life.

Identify the Cause

Explore why you feel stressed and the source of this stress. It may be possible to address the source of stress in your life. Even if you cannot alleviate the stress, you can develop a plan for minimizing it.

Monitor Moods

Try to determine when, where, and why you are feeling stressed. This can help you identify stressful situations so you can take steps to address or avoid them.

Give Yourself Time

Personal time can allow you to take a step back from stressful situations and rejuvenate. Consider taking a few minutes several times a day. Set aside longer periods several times a week.

Use this time to relax, meditate, exercise, look at a magazine, or engage in some other form of mental "escape".

Manage Anger

Employ anger management techniques such as counting to ten or taking a walk, in order to avoid emotional outbursts, which can greatly increase stress.

Consider your Priorities

An overly full schedule and too many responsibilities can create stress. Review your responsibilities and prioritize them, consider delegating or eliminating those that are less important.

Cut Yourself some Slack

Perfectionists are often very stressed-out people. Set reasonable standards for yourself and others.

Source: American Psychological Association, www.apa.org

- **Seek Professional Support**
  Many mental health and addiction professionals find it beneficial to participate in support groups designed specifically for "helping" professionals. Others benefit from individual sessions with a therapist. Just because you spend all day helping others, it doesn't mean that you cannot benefit from help.

Resources

American Psychological Association Help Center
APA's Help Center provides brochures, tips, and articles on the psychological issues that affect physical and emotional well-being and provides information about referrals.

National Institute of Mental Health
Includes information on research and treatment of mental health disorders and provides resources related to mental wellness, including a services locator.

Substance Abuse and Mental Health Services Administration (SAMHSA), Center for Mental Health Services
Information on mental health, including a treatment locator.

4. Recovery Management

Research indicates that approximately 60 percent of addiction professionals are in recovery (CSAT, 2006). This translates into a significant workplace issue: how to keep people in recovery when they work in an environment where they are constantly coming into contact with current and former addicts. Addiction professionals may also adopt the attitude that because of their professional background, they are better prepared to avoid relapse than other people in recovery. These factors, coupled with the already stressful environment in which addiction professionals work, make recovery management a crucial issue for both agencies and employees.

Agencies have adopted different approaches to addressing recovery. Some choose to have specific activities for people in recovery, such as onsite support groups or providing flex time to attend meetings. Other agencies incorporate recovery management into their overall wellness activities and do not provide specific services for employees in recovery.

Possible Signs of Relapse

- Change in work attendance or performance
- Alteration of personal appearance
- Mood swings or attitude changes
- Withdrawal from responsibility or contact with associates
- Unusual patterns of behavior
- Defensive attitude concerning addiction

Resources

Recovery Community Services Program

This is a SAMHSA-supported program in which peer-to-peer recovery support services are provided to help people initiate and/ or sustain recovery from alcohol and drug use disorders.

Faces & Voices of Recovery

Faces & Voices of Recovery is a national organization of individuals and organizations coming together to support local, state, regional and national recovery advocacy by increasing access to research, policy, organizing, and technical support; facilitating relationships among local and regional groups; improving access to policymakers and the media; and providing a national rallying point for recovery advocates.

National Drug Addiction Recovery Month

The *Recovery Month* effort aims to promote the societal benefits of alcohol and drug use disorder treatment, laud the contributions of treatment providers and promote the message that recovery from alcohol and drug use disorders in all its forms is possible.

WORKING AS AN ADDICTION PROFESSIONAL IS NOT A PLAN OF PERSONAL RECOVERY

A fundamental principle of all 12-step and many faith-based addiction recovery programs is a belief that a person in "continuous-sustained recovery" must commit to working with others in "early recovery" in order to maintain their own individual sobriety or "clean time". This principle is referred to as "12-step or service work," and is often characterized by the phrase "you can only keep what you have by giving it away." This practice can be traced to AA's co-founder Bill Wilson and one of his early experiences. One evening, after experiencing a severe urge to drink, Mr. Wilson frantically began phoning local Akron, OH, hospitals in search of a "suffering alcoholic" with whom he could share his "road to recovery" experiences.

Mr. Wilson believed that in order for him to overcome his urge to drink and to remain sober, he would have to "work with others" who were struggling to find sobriety. Some 53 years later, this practice continues to be a mainstay of the addiction recovery community. It is a fundamental principle highlighted throughout the 12th step of most, if not all, "anonymous" programs.

Addiction professionals who are also members of the addiction recovery community must be careful not to confuse their work as professional addiction counselors with their commitment to "service work."

So often, many among this group mistake their professional work with service work. Working as an addiction professional does not constitute a program of personal recovery. This error in judgment can be costly, resulting in a disconnect from their personal support system and possibly leading to relapse to substance use.

A common sign suggesting the possible blurring of this fine line can be found in comments such as: "I don't have to go to meetings any more because I work with newcomers daily in my profession as a counselor," or "I keep what I have through my work as an addiction counselor."

Being employed in treatment is not the same as, "working with newcomers." One is a profession; the other a livelihood. For the protection of those who are in recovery and employed as treatment professionals, this understanding must be made clear. It may be the difference between a long and prosperous career and a return to active addiction, or worse, death, since relapse can also be fatal.

David Whiters
Executive Director, Recovery Consultants of Atlanta, Inc.

SECTION 4. LOSS AND GRIEF

Goal of Section:
Identify how grief may manifest itself in the emotional and behavioral responses of individuals

The experience of loss is common in the field of addiction. Our clients often experience overwhelming loss as a result of dealing with complex issues in their lives. Relapse and loss as a result of overdose, interpersonal or community violence, unemployment, illness, incarceration, suicide or homicide are more commonplace within the field of addiction than in other professions. As a consequence, many addiction professionals don't discuss the impact of client, co-worker and personal loss on their professional practice and overall well-being. It is important to understand how regular, continuous loss impacts professional practice and overall well-being.

Loss versus Grief

Loss is being deprived of something one has had or hopes to have, but does not attain. Grief is the process of understanding and accepting loss. The process occurs over time. It is highly individualized and varies depending on what is being grieved by whom, when and where. There is a grief reaction for every loss including death. Some losses are minor and grief is manageable. Other losses may be more significant leading to depression or an extended grief response.

The 4 Types of Loss

- Natural – Anticipated
- Unpredictable – Natural Disasters
- Human induced – Accidental
- Human induced – Deliberate Violence

Natural – Sometimes Anticipated

- Death after prolonged illness
- Incarceration
- Job loss
- Loss of mobility
- Relapse

Some loss is natural and anticipated. Although you hoped for improvement, you realized that loss was on the horizon. In this type of loss you are able to anticipate a negative outcome. However despite the fact that you were able to prepare for the loss, you experienced feelings of dread and uncertainty. You felt like you are on a rollercoaster. At times you believed there would be a positive outcome only to have your hopes dashed at a later time.

Unpredictable-Natural Disasters

- Earthquake
- Fire
- Flood
- Storm
- Tornado

Some loss is the result of an unpredictable, natural disaster. Your world can be shattered and broken apart by natural, unexpected and unpredictable loss. Although we hear about these events happening to others, we never expect them to happen to us. It is especially difficult when death is involved. The unpredictable nature allowed no time to prepare or say goodbye. loss. Although we hear about these events happening to others, we never expect them to happen to us. It is especially difficult when death is involved. The unpredictable nature allowed no time to prepare or say goodbye.

Human Induced – Accidental

- Automobile accident
- Clinical or medical error

Human induced, accidental loss is also unexpected. An accident or mistake results in a terrible loss. The complication from this type of loss is that someone is to blame. This type of loss may involve co-workers, other clients, law enforcement, the courts, insurance companies and other parties.

Human Induced – Deliberate

- Arson
- Assault
- Rape
- Murder
- Suicide

Human induced, deliberate violence is the result of deliberate intent to cause harm to self or another person. It may seem impossible to understand why someone would purposely create the situation resulting in loss. This type of loss is further complicated by fear for personal safety and those for whom you provide services.

Grief

6 Facts about Grief

1. We grieve all losses.
2. Grief is more than an emotional experience. It is also experienced as a physical, psychological, spiritual and behavioral reactions.
3. We cannot control where we grieve or what will trigger grief.
4. Grief is an uneven process with no timeline.
5. Grieving means going on with our life; while maintaining memories, connections, and feelings of grief and loss.
6. Over time, most people learn to live with loss.

Common Immediate Reactions to Grief

- Emotional: Feelings of shock and relief
- Physical: Shortness of breath, numbness, listlessness, feeling empty, chest pain, loss of energy, and confusion
- Cognitive and Behavioral: Denial, disorientation

Common Reactions after the Shock

- Emotional: Anger, fear, guilt, panic, loneliness, depression
- Physical: Lack of energy, chestpains, fatigue, tension
- Behavioral: sleeplessness and withdrawal or sleeping too much, overeating, substance use such as sleep aids, drugs, alcohol

Professional Grief

Working in a high loss environment is stressful. There is an expectation that those who work in high loss environments will adapt and that it will become easier to accept loss. To function adequately during times of crisis, the addiction professional learns to set aside personal emotions. Professional grief is internalized and overshadowed by the demands of work. It is important to note that loss and resulting grief is experienced regardless of whether or not it is outwardly expressed. Over time cumulative unexpressed grief can lead to vulnerability, burnout, compassion fatigue or post-traumatic stress reaction.

Characteristics of Professioal Grief

- Regular, continuous professiona loss
- Grief may be chronic or delayed
- Aloof and distant mourner
- Grief transformed into other emotions such as anger, anxiety, blame, helplessness & guilt
- Cumulative, unexpressed grief results in vulnerability, burnout, compassion fatigue or post-traumatic stress syndrome

Denying the significance of the loss can make grief harder and can extend the grief process. Another concern is that most individuals and their families don't know what to expect with acute grief. They become concerned that what they or family members are experiencing isn't normal.

Maintaining Professional Balance

When working in a high loss environment, there is a need to maintain a balance between engagement and detachment. When the balance is lost, detachment of engagement can become dysfunctional. This may result in an inability to meet your needs or those of your clients.

Signs of Imbalance in Professional Grief

- Decrease in tolerance or sensitivity
- Cynicism regarding your work and that of others
- Difficulty maintaining hope at work and in your personal life.

FOUR MAJOR TASKS

- Accepting the Reality of the Loss
- Experiencing the Pain of Grief
- Adjusting to a Changed Enviroment
- Going Forward Emotionally

---

10 TIPS FOR MAINTAING BALANCE

1. Reach out for support from your peers, friends and families.
2. Remember that you don't have to be a hero and go it alone.
3. Create opportunities to debrief, and use professional counseling when appropriate.
4. Be kind to yourself and have fun.
5. Remember that you don't have to — and can't! — be perfect.
6. Stay healthy through restorative self-care and remember to laugh.
7. Set healthy boundaries.
8. Acknowledge your own woundedness, and use it to be an empathic source of wisdom.
9. Create rituals to delineate work time from personal time.
10. Reflect on powerful or difficult experiences through journaling and the support of peers, spiritual teachers and mentors to recover a sense of meaning, purpose and connection in life.

APPENDICES

Sample Retreat Agenda

Annual Staff Retreat

AGENDA

9:30 am   Continental Breakfast
9:50 am   Welcome and overview of AGENDA
             Overview of Retreat

a. What is a retreat?
b. Why are we having a retreat?
c. What we plan to accomplish.

10:30 am	History of the Organization
11:15 am	Board of Directors Presentation
	Getting-to-Know-You Exercise, Facilitated by Board members
12:00 pm	Lunch
12:45 pm	Strategies for improving overall mental, physical and spiritual health of staff – with special emphasis on recovering staff
2:00 pm	Strategies for improving overall effectiveness of staff
3:00 pm	Review, feedback and completion of evaluations
3:30 pm	Adjourn

Smoking Cessation

In 2006, 45.1 million adults (20.8%) in the United States were current smokers: 23.6 percent of men and 18.1 percent of women. An estimated 70 percent of these smokers said they wanted to quit (National Center for Health Statistics, 2006). Smoking has been linked to numerous diseases including: abdominal aortic aneurysm; acute myeloid leukemia; cancer (bladder, cervical, esophageal, kidney, laryngeal, lung, oral, pancreatic, stomach, and throat); cardiovascular diseases; cataract; chronic lung diseases; coronary heart; pneumonia; and periodontitis. Smoke from other people's cigarettes, known as secondhand smoke, also causes lung cancer (U.S. Department of Health and Human Services, 2004).

It is no secret that many people with addictions to alcohol and other drugs are also smokers, there is a very high rate of co-addiction (Anthony & Wagner, 2000). Current research has also begun to suggest that smoking is a predictor of alcohol and substance abuse (McKee, Falba, O'Malley, Sindelar, & O'Connor, 2007). This means that many people in recovery also smoke. While they have been able stop drinking or using drugs, many continue to smoke.

Ask anyone who has tried, quitting smoking is not easy. Studies have shown that there are specific steps to quitting smoking. These include: preparing (readiness); identifying support; learning new skills and behaviors; getting medication if necessary; and preparing for relapse.

If you are thinking about quitting, consider attempting it at a time when stress levels are low. It could be too much to take on during times of financial, work-related, or relationship stress.

Also consider a visit to your physician if you are thinking about quitting. Physicians can suggest medicine to help with withdrawal, some of which can be purchased over the counter while others require a prescription. There are also programs and support groups available to help people stop smoking.

Resources

Smokefree.gov
This HHS site includes an online guide to quitting.
www.smokefree.gov

Tobacco Information and Prevention Source (TIPS)
CDC website that includes resources on prevention and smoking cessation.
www.cdc.gov/tobacco

American Lung Association
www.lungusa.org/site/pp.asp?c=dvLUK9O0E&b=22931

Dr. Jeff's Quit Commit Program for Smoking Cessation
This user friendly website helps people of all ages to quit smoking cigarettes.
www.quitcommit.com

Stress Style Test

Created by Daniel Goleman, PhD

Imagine yourself in a stressful situation. When you are feeling anxious, what do you typically experience? Check all that apply.

1. My heart beats faster.
2. I find it difficult to concentrate because of distracting thoughts.
3. I worry too much about things that don't really matter.
4. I feel jittery.

5. I get diarrhea.
6. I imagine terrifying scenes.
7. I can't keep anxiety-provoking pictures and images out of my mind.
8. My stomach gets tense.
9. I pace up and down nervously.
10. I am bothered by unimportant thoughts running through my mind.
11. I become immobilized.
12. I feel I am losing out on things because I can't make decisions fast enough.
13. I perspire.
14. I can't stop thinking worrisome thoughts.

Give yourself a "mind" point if you checked the following questions: 2, 3, 6, 7, 10, 12, and 14.

Mind Total: _____

Give yourself a "body" point if you checked the following questions: 1, 4, 5, 8, 9, 11, and 13.

Body Total: _____

Choosing a Relaxer

Body

If stress registers mainly in your body, you will need a remedy that will break up the physical tension pattern. This may be a vigorous body workout but a slow-paced, even lazy, muscle relaxer may be equally effective. Here are some suggestions.

Aerobics
Progressive relaxation
Swimming
Biking
Rowing
Running
Walking
Yoga
Massage
Soaking in a hot tub

Deep Breathing
Golf

Mind

If you experience stress as an invasion of worrisome thoughts, the most direct intervention is anything that will engage your mind completely and redirect it, such as meditation. On the other hand, some people find that the sheer exertion of physical exercise unhooks the mind wonderfully and is very effective therapy. Here are some suggestions.

Meditation
Exercise
Reading
Crosswords, puzzles
TV, movies
Games, such as chess and cards
Knitting and sewing
Carpentry, handicrafts
Any absorbing hobby
Creative imagery

Mind/Body

If you are a mixed type, you may want to try a physical activity that also demands mental rigor.

Competitive sports (tennis, racquetball, squash, volleyball)
Any combination of mind and body activity

Coping Index

1. If you have a supportive family, give yourself 10 points
2. If you pursue a hobby at least 1–2 hours a week, give yourself 10 points.
3. If you attend a social activity at least once per week, give yourself 10 points.
4. If you are within 15 pounds of your ideal weight, give yourself 15 points.

5. If you do at least 90 minutes of deep relaxation or meditation per week, give yourself 10 points.
6. For each day per week you perform at least 30 minutes of aerobic exercise, give yourself 5 points.
7. For each balanced meal you eat per day, give yourself 5 points (figure your average day, up to a total of 15 points)
8. If you do at least one activity per week "just for you," give yourself 10 points.
9. If you have a place in your home where you can relax without interruptions, give yourself 10 points.
10. If you use a time management program or process regularly, give yourself 10 points.
11. For each pack of cigarettes that you smoke per day, subtract 10 points.
12. For each day per week you use a form of medication to relax, subtract 5 points.
13. For each day per week that you drink alcohol, subtract 5 points.
14. For each day per week that you use alcohol to help you relax, subtract 10 points.
15. For each day per week that you take work home, subtract 5 points (up to 35 points).

Total

Coping Index Scale

0–25 points	Heading for serious trouble. Stress illnesses and/or burnout may be already happening or are imminent.
25–55 points	Index is still problematic. Some illnesses are likely.
56 points or higher	A healthy stress index. Good reserves for managing stress.

Compassion Satisfaction/Fatigue Self-Test for Helpers[1]

Helping others puts you in direct contact with other people's lives. As you probably have experienced, your compassion for those you help has both positive and negative aspects. This self-test helps you estimate your compassion status: how much at risk you are of burnout and compassion fatigue and also the degree of satisfaction with helping others. Consider each of the following characteristics about you and your current situation. Write in the number that honestly reflects how frequently you experienced these characteristics in the last week. Then follow the scoring directions at the end of the self-test.

0=Never 1=Rarely 2=A Few Times 3=Somewhat Often 4=Often 5=Very Often

Items about You

1. I am happy.
2. I find my life satisfying.
3. I have beliefs that sustain me.
4. I feel estranged from others.
5. I find that I learn new things from those I care for.
6. I force myself to avoid certain thoughts or feelings that remind me of a frightening experience.
7. I find myself avoiding certain activities or situations because they remind me of a frightening experience.
8. I have gaps in my memory about frightening events.
9. I feel connected to others.
10. I feel calm.
11. I believe that I have a good balance between my work and my free time.
12. I have difficulty falling or staying asleep.
13. I have outbursts of anger or irritability with little provocation.
14. I am the person I always wanted to be.
15. I startle easily.
16. While working with a victim, I thought about violence against the perpetrator.
17. I am a sensitive person.
18. I have flashbacks connected to those I help.
19. I have good peer support when I need to work through a highly stressful experience.
20. I have had first-hand experience with traumatic events in my adult life.
21. I have had first-hand experience with traumatic events in my childhood.
22. I think that I need to "work through" a traumatic experience in my life.
23. I think that I need more close friends.

24. I think that there is no one to talk with about highly stressful experiences.
25. I have concluded that I work too hard for my own good.
26. Working with those I help brings me a great deal of satisfaction.
27. I feel invigorated after working with those I help.
28. I am frightened of things a person I helped has said or done to me.
29. I experience troubling dreams similar to those I help.
30. I have happy thoughts about those I help and how I could help them.
31. I have experienced intrusive thoughts of times with especially difficult people I helped.
32. I have suddenly and involuntarily recalled a frightening experience while working with a person I helped.
33. I am pre-occupied with more than one person I help.
34. I am losing sleep over a person I help's traumatic experiences.
35. I have joyful feelings about how I can help the victims I work with.
36. I think that I might have been "infected" by the traumatic stress of those I help.
37. I think that I might be positively "inoculated" by the traumatic stress of those I help.
38. I remind myself to be less concerned about the well-being of those I help.
39. I have felt trapped by my work as a helper.
40. I have a sense of hopelessness associated with working with those I help.
41. I have felt "on edge" about various things and I attribute this to working with certain people I help.
42. I wish that I could avoid working with some people I help.
43. Some people I help are particularly enjoyable to work with.
44. I have been in danger working with people I help.
45. I feel that some people I help dislike me personally.

0=Never 1=Rarely 2=A Few Times 3=Somewhat Often 4=Often 5=Very Often

Items about being a Helper and Your Helping Environment

46. I like my work as a helper.
47. I feel like I have the tools and resources that I need to do my work as a helper.

48. I have felt weak, tired, run down as a result of my work as helper.
49. I have felt depressed as a result of my work as a helper.
50. I have thoughts that I am a "success" as a helper.
51. I am unsuccessful at separating helping from personal life.
52. I enjoy my co-workers.
53. I depend on my co-workers to help me when I need it.
54. My co-workers can depend on me for help when they need it.
55. I trust my co-workers.
56. I feel little compassion toward most of my co-workers.
57. I am pleased with how I am able to keep up with helping technology.
58. I feel I am working more for the money/prestige than for personal fulfillment.
59. Although I have to do paperwork that I don't like, I still have time to work with those I help.
60. I find it difficult separating my personal life from my helper life.
61. I am pleased with how I am able to keep up with helping techniques and protocols.
62. I have a sense of worthlessness/disillusionment/resentment associated with my ole as a helper.
63. I have thoughts that I am a "failure" as a helper.
64. I have thoughts that I am not succeeding at achieving my life goals.
65. I have to deal with bureaucratic, unimportant tasks in my work as a helper.
66. I plan to be a helper for a long time.

Self-Test Scoring Instructions

Please note that research is ongoing on this scale and the following scores should be used as a guide, not confirmatory information.

1. Be certain you respond to all items.
2. Mark the items for scoring:
   a. Put an x by the following 26 items: 1–3, 5, 9–11, 14, 19, 26–27, 30, 35, 37, 43, 46–47, 50, 52–55, 57, 59, 61, 66.
   b. Put a check by the following 16 items: 17, 23–25, 41, 42, 45, 48, 49, 51, 56, 58, 60, 62–65.
   c. Circle the following 23 items: 4, 6–8, 12, 13, 15, 16, 18, 20–22, 28, 29, 31–34, 36, 38–40, and 44.
3. Add the numbers you wrote next to the items for each set of items and note:

Your potential for Compassion Satisfaction (x):
118 and above = extremely high potential
100–117 = high potential
82–99 = good potential
64–81 = modest potential
below 63 = low potential

Your risk for Burnout (check):
32 or less = extremely low risk
33–37= low risk
34–50 = moderate risk
51–75 = high risk
76–85 = extremely high risk

Your risk for Compassion Fatigue (circle):
26 or less = extremely low risk
27–30 = low risk
31–35 = moderate risk
36–40 = high risk
41 or more = extremely high risk

Chart by circling the appropriate score categories below for your assessed level of risk.

Level of Risk	Burnout Level	Compassion Fatigue (CF) Level	Satisfaction Level
High/Extremely High	51 or more	36 or more	82 or more
Moderate	34 – 50	31 – 35	64 – 81
Extremely Low/Low	32 or less	30 or less	63 or less

REFERENCES

Aldana, S. G. (2001). Financial impact of health promotion programs: A comprehensive review of the literature. *American Journal of Health Promotion, 15*(5), 296–320.

Anthony, J. & Wagner, F. (2000). Epidemiologic analysis of alcohol and tobacco use. *Alcohol Research & Health, 24*(4), 201–208.

Bride, B. E., Robinson, M. M., Yegidis, B. & Figley, C. R. (2003). *Development and validation of the secondary trauma stress scale. Research on Social Work Practice, 13,* 1-16.

Center for Substance Abuse Treatment. (1995). S*creening for infectious diseases among substance abusers.* Treatment Improvement Protocol (TIP) Series, Number 6. Publication No. (SMA) 95-3060. Rockville, MD: CSAT.

Center for Substance Abuse Treatment. (2002). *Addiction counseling competencies: The knowledge, skills, and attitudes of professional practice.* Technical Assistance Publication (TAP) Series, Number 21. DHHS Publication No. (SMA) 02-3625. Rockville, MD: CSAT.

Center for Substance Abuse Treatment. (2006). *Substance abuse: Administrative issues in outpatient treatment.* Treatment Improvement Protocol (TIP) Series, Number 46. DHHS Publication No. (SMA) 06-4151. Rockville, MD: CSAT.

Centers for Disease Control and Prevention. (2006). *National Health and Nutrition Examination Survey Report.* Retrieved May 23, 2009, from: www. cdc.gov/nchs/data/databriefs/db01.pdf

Figley, C. R. (1985). The family as victim: Mental health implications. *Psychiatry, 6,* 283–291.

Hoge, M. A., Morris, J. A., Daniels, A. S., Huey, L. Y., Stuart, G. W. Adams, N. et al. (2005). Report of recommendations: The Annapolis Coalition Conference on Behavioral Health Work Force Competencies. *Administration and Policy in Mental Health, 32*(5), 651–663.

Institute of Medicine (IOM) (2004). *Keeping patients safe: Transforming the work environment of nurses.* Washington, DC: The National Academies Press.

McKee, S. A., Falba T., O'Malley, S. S., Sindelar, J. & O'Connor, P. G. (2007). Smoking status as a clinical indicator for alcohol misuse in U. S. adults. *Archives of Internal Medicine, 167*(7), 716–721.

McLellan, A. T., Carise, D. & Kleber, H. D. (2003). Can the national addiction treatment infrastructure support the public's demand for quality care? *Journal of Substance Abuse Treatment, 25*(2) 117–121.

Miller, W. R. (1998). Researching the spiritual dimensions of alcohol and other drug problems. *Addictions, 93*(7), 979–990.

Moody, E. E. (2010). *First aid for your emotional hurts: Grief.* Nashville, TN: Randall House.

National Center for Health Statistics (2006). *Health, United States, 2008 with CHARTBOOK.* Retrieved May 27, 2009 from: www.cdc.gov/nchs/ data/hus/hus08.pdf#063.

National Institute of Mental Health (2007). *Statistics.* Retrieved May 23, 2007, from: www.nimh.nih.gov/healthinformation/statisticsmenu.cfm.

Parkes, C. M. (1986). *Orienteering the caregiver's grief. Journal of Palliative Care, 1,* 5-7.

Powell, D. J. & Brodsky, A. (2004). *Clinical supervision in alcohol and drug abuse counseling: Principles, models, methods* (Rev. Ed.) Hoboken, NJ: Jossey-Bass.

Rothschild, B. & Rand, M. (2006). *Help for the helper: The psychophysiology of compassion fatigue and vicarious trauma.* New York: W. W. Norton & Company.

U. S. Department of Health and Human Services & U. S. Department of Agriculture. (2005). *Dietary guidelines for americans.* Washington, DC: Government Printing Office.

End Note

[1] Adopted by B. Stamm and included in a chapter in C. R. Figley (Ed.) (in press), Treating Compassion Fatigue. Philadelphia: Brunner/Mazel.

INDEX

S